John Ewer

A sermon preached before the incorporated Society for the

Propagation of the Gospel in Foreign Parts

At their anniversary meeting in the parish church of St. Mary-le-Bow, on Friday,

February 20, 1767

John Ewer

A sermon preached before the incorporated Society for the Propagation of the Gospel in Foreign Parts
At their anniversary meeting in the parish church of St. Mary-le-Bow, on Friday, February 20, 1767

ISBN/EAN: 9783337713881

Printed in Europe, USA, Canada, Australia, Japan

Cover: Foto ©ninafisch / pixelio.de

More available books at **www.hansebooks.com**

A

S E R M O N

Preached before the

Incorporated S O C I E T Y

F O R   T H E

Propagation of the Gospel in Foreign Parts;

A T   T H E I R

ANNIVERSARY MEETING

I N   T H E

Parish Church of St. Mary-le-Bow,

On F R I D A Y *February* 20, 1767.

By the Right Reverend Father in G O D,
J O H N Lord Bishop of *L A N D A F F.*

L O N D O N:
Printed by E. Owen and T. Harrison in
Warwick-Lane.
MDCCLXVII.

At the Anniversary Meeting of the Society for the Propagation of the Gospel in Foreign Parts, *in the* Vestry-Room *of St*. Mary-le-Bow, *on* Friday *the* 20*th Day of* February, 1767.

AGREED, that the Thanks of the SOCIETY be given to the Right Reverend the Lord Bishop of *Landaff*, for his Sermon preached this Day before the SOCIETY; and that his Lordship be desired to deliver a Copy of the same to the SOCIETY to be Printed.

Daniel Burton, Secretary.

Epiftle to the ROMANS, chap. x.
Part of the 14th verfe.

*How shall they believe in him, of whom
they have not heard? And how shall
they hear without a Preacher?*

AN comes into the world,
endowed with certain in-
ftincts for the prefervation of
himfelf and of his kind. This
inftinctive knowledge, common to him with the brute
creation, he receives from nature, perfect and
intire without difcipline or ftudy; and this is
the only knowledge he fo receives, of neceffity
and not of choice. All higher qualities, that
adorn and diftinguifh men from beafts, are not

A 2   im-

implanted by nature, but to be acquired. Arts,
fciences, morality and religion are all of this
condition: we are born not with the knowledge of them, but with a capacity only of
knowing them. The communication of arts
and fciences from people to people may be
traced; and in places where they flourifh, we
fee them delivered from age to age by education. Morality and religion, notwithftanding
man's natural capacity to underftand them, yet
have not in fact, by the mere ftrength of nature, been any where rightly underftood: witnefs, before the Propagation of the Gofpel, one
family excepted, the whole race of mankind:
witnefs, fince the Propagation of it, all people
who have continued heathen; thofe efpecially,
whom we purchafe as cattle with our money,
and having fo purchafed, treat as cattle; and that
other race of favages, our neighbours in America. Thefe untutored people we experimen-
tally know to be ignorant of arts and fciences,
of morality, of God. Much lefs can revealed
religion be known without teaching. This is
evident to common fenfe, and demonftrated by
the example of the Jews; who lived in grofs
ignorance of their law, and were ever revolting
from God to idols for a courfe of many ages;
until

until means were provided for a general and frequent instruction of the people in their revelation: but when synagogues for that purpose were at length erected throughout their dwellings, the same people, before so prone to revolt, did thenceforward, by virtue of a regular instruction in their law, adhere faithfully and invariably to the one true God, Creator of heaven and earth.

Whatever is knowable only by instruction, can no otherwise be preserved in the knowledge of successive generations, than by successive and continued instruction. And need I say, that Christian doctrine is a doctrine of this kind, not born with us, nor the unavoidable result of reason; but necessary to be learned and to be maintained by perpetual teaching and hearing? Wherefore it was necessary, that an order of men, with perpetual succession, should be ordained and dedicated to the service of preaching the Gospel, as the only means of gaining it a first reception in any place, of preserving it where received, and of spreading it thence wider and still wider; if it was designed, as hath frequently been demonstrated on this occasion, to be universal in extent, and permanent in duration. For this end our Saviour

sent

fent forth his apoftles; the apoftles commif-
fioned new teachers, with power of delivering
down the fame commiffion to others; and thus
was appointed a fucceffion of minifters to the
end of the world.   In confequence of this appointment, and the neceffity of the thing, a
ftanding miniftry hath at all times been maintained in all Chriftian countries.

This hath been done in all ordinary cafes;
but in extraordinary cafes, fuch as have frequently happened fince the difcovery of the
new world, the fame provifion hath not been
made of minifters, neceffary to the fupport of
Chriftianity among thofe who removed thither;
efpecially in the Britifh colonies; a fcandalous
neglect, which hath brought great and deferved reproach both on the adventurers, and
on the government whence they went; and
under whofe protection and power they ftill re-
mained in their new habitations.

Upon the adventurers what reproach could
be caft, heavier than they deferved? Who,
with their native foil, abandoned their native manners and religion; and e'er long,
were found in many parts living without re-
membrance or knowledge of God, without
any divine worfhip, in diffolute wickednefs,
                                                        and

and the moſt brutal profligacy of manners. Inſtead of civilizing and converting barbarous Infidels, as they undertook to do, they became themſelves Infidels and Barbarians. And is it not ſome aggravation of their ſhame, that this their neglect of religion was contrary to the pretences and conditions, under which they obtained royal grants and public authority to their adventures? The pretences and conditions were, that their deſign was, and that they ſhould endeavour, the enlargement of commerce, and the propagation of Chriſtian faith : the former they executed with ſincerity and zeal; in the latter moſt notoriouſly failed.

Their failure herein might well have been expected : religion and traffic, their two pro-feſſed objects, are but ill yoke-fellows, being apt to draw quite different ways : and men, who with deſperate hardineſs invade unknown difficulties and dangers in queſt of gain, could not be ſuppoſed to be much concerned about ſpiritual intereſts. Religion is but an impedi-ment in the way of avarice : many things thereby prohibited, are deemed allowable, and ſtick cloſe to traffic. Commerce indeed has been the occaſion of communicating the know-ledge of Chriſt from nation to nation; but perſons

engaged

engaged therein have not been the communicators of it, their bufinefs is of another fort. But this hath been done by other men, detached from worldly affairs, and zealous and fkilful in divine knowledge; who taking advantage of the intercourfe opened by them with other views, have preached the Gofpel where it was before unknown. In this way our Planters have excelled, having given double occafion of propagating Chriftianity among the native heathen of thofe regions, and among themfelves alfo, who foon became heathen.

As this their defection could not but have been forefeen, if regarded; and being forefeen, might have been prevented; upon that account, the greater reproach hath but too juftly been caft upon the government of thofe times; which either was wholly inattentive to a matter of that importance, or faw it with indifference. In a Chriftian ftate confidered as Chriftian, fuch indifference is altogether prodigious; confidered in a temporal view, fuch indifference to religion argues indifference to the public good, or want of wifdom and found policy. It argues ignorance of the nature of men the fubjects of government, of the power of confcience, and the influence of human hopes and fears.

fears. It argues ignorance of the foundation of thofe qualities, without which fociety cannot be fafe, truth, juftice and fidelity, which ftand on the foundation of religion, and can ftand firm on no other foundation whatever. It argues ignorance of the practice of all ftates in all ages, or elfe an incapacity to underftand the reafon of the practice: for what government ever exifted on earth, that had no religion? What legiflator, who introduced not fome kind of it? So advantageous hath it ever been found to ftates, that, for this very reafon, the enemies of religion, and thereby the enemies of mankind, have plaufibly pretended, that having no foundation in nature, it is the mere invention of ftatefmen. Perverfe inference! becaufe religion is adapted to human nature, therefore not from God. This adaption, this mutual agreement and harmony between them, is, among many, one convincing argument, that they proceed from one common author, and are both from God. However the neceffity of religion to ftates being acknowledged, and the benefit thereof to individuals apparent; it is hard to fay, both in regard to the ftate and to the people, whether the neglect of it in our colonies were more

B impolitic

impolitic in point of worldly judgment, or
more impious in the eftimation of piety; fince
irreligion is equally offenfive to heaven, and
deftructive of worldly happinefs.

Now this great evil, irreligion, might at
firft have eafily been prevented growing in our
colonies: but the fame evil having been fuffered to grow, hath been found fo hard to expel, that now, after more than fixty years diligent endeavour, it is very far from being era-
dicated. Confider then the danger of this evil
how great; the prevention of it how eafy; the
remedy how difficult and flow. Confider its rife
and progrefs in the old plantations; new ones,
in the late conquefts, are now making, and
more are likely to be made. The fore-men-
tioned confiderations are therefore feafonable,
and demand the fpecial attention of all leaders
of colonies; who henceforward, if they repeat
the fame error, will err inexcufably, againft
warning, againft example, againft the experience of former generations; whofe meafures,
wherein wife, do beft point out to pofterity
the right path; wherein erroneous, do moft
ftrongly dehort from the wrong. This great
advantage of former experience is now held
forth, and in a manner forced upon all perfons.
The

The rocks on which their predeceffors in this way fplit, ftand marked out : the ruinous con-fequences of their mifconduct ftill reft upon us, ftill remain manifeft, and are likely long to remain. If men will but open their eyes, they muft fee, that prudence as well as piety requires, that provifion for religion make a part in the original conftitution of every co-lony : if they will not fee nor perform what private intereft and duty perfuade ; the public eye doubtlefs will be open, and public autho-rity exact the performance of what fo effen-tially concerns the common weal. And can there be a doubt, that this provifion ought to be made by the care, and at the expence of the colonifts if able? If unable through poverty, and they, on that account, receive public affiftance in fettling themfelves, the national intereft plain-ly requires, that they fhould receive public affift-ance alfo in fettling religion among them : for who would have for fubjects a band of men with-out any ? Nor is it juft or fafe, that this bur-then fhould be thrown on a charity, upon which greater demands, than can be anfwered, are already made. Befides, provifion for reli-gion ought to be certain and permanent ; but the fund of this Corporation, depending upon free contributions, is uncertain and precarious.

In

In the old plantations, failures in this kind
feem to have proceeded rather from want of
good will than of ability; for though many
neglected, fome took effectual care of this bufinefs. Confcientious perfons, who left their
country, on religious motives, did fo: others,
who were led abroad merely by a prevailing
thirft, and eager hope of gain, left religion to
fhift for itfelf. Future emigrants muft be of
this latter kind: (for who now will leave this
country on a religious account) fuch perfons,
it is evident, are not fit to be trufted with the
care of religion; nor will it be fufficient to
make it a condition in their grants, that with
themfelves they fhall at the fame time fettle
religion among them; for that claufe hath
been ever confidered as matter of mere form.
Wherefore it will moreover be neceffary that
they be obferved, watched, and by authority
obliged effectually to perform that condition.
Whoever then fhall employ his care, his coun-
fel or authority, as opportunity may ferve, to
procure due regulations in thefe and the like
matters, will difcharge the office of a good
Member of this Society; for to prevent the
rife of irreligion in new plantations is one way,
and the beft way, of anfwering the ends thereof;
it being, in all cafes, far better, as well as

eafier,

eafier, to fhut the gates againft the entrance of an enemy, than to expel him, if that be practicable, after he has got entrance and poffeffion.

Now the prevention, or removal of irreligion, and of falfe religion, with their long train of attendant mifchiefs, can no otherwife be effected, than by propagating the pure doctrines revealed from heaven. If it can be done by any other means, it muft be by reafon; or, in other words, by philofophy, which is, or pretends to be, the higheft improvement of reafon. What philofophy can do, may be beft eftimated by what it hath done. Now that philofophy never did, in any age or country, teach, or attempt to teach, the bulk of mankind right notions concerning God, divine worfhip, and moral obligation, is, I apprehend, a fact, that cannot be controverted. To their actual teaching thefe points, there was an infuperable obftacle, *viz.* they themfelves were in the dark about them. To the attempt there were feveral difcouragements; it was dangerous; and the vulgar were neither capable of learning, nor of paying their mafters. However, therefore, fome philofophers might perchance have formed, in their own minds, better

ter

ter notions than were vulgarly entertained; yet no information redounded from them to the body of the people. Their doctrines, whatever they were, were taught to a few followers, men of leisure in their respective schools; or sometimes perhaps discussed before Princes and great men, admirers of curious and subtle speculations; or delivered, with quaint and abstracted refinements, in books which mean and illiterate people had neither leisure to read, nor capacity to understand. Hence it happened, in ages when philosophy was best cultivated, and carried to its utmost height, that an universal ignorance of the one true supreme God, of his attributes, and of his worship, prevailed in all nations: and for this universal ignorance of divine things, the philosophers had in store no adequate remedy; nor did they attempt generally to apply any partial and imperfect remedy, they had perhaps discovered. Thus, during the empire of philosophy, stood the knowledge of divine things in the world. As to the rules of morality laid down by wise men of old, they are, without doubt, as far as they reach, good, just, and of admirable use; yet, in some respects, fall short of the evangelical precepts. This indeed is one, but the least

defect

defect in them. It is a greater, that the teachers being invested with no authority, their dictates were disputable; every one thought he had a right to reject them if he pleased, and to oppose his own reason to that of another man. But the greatest defect was this; that, by their deepest researches, they could find no firm ground, whereon to fix any sure obligation to the observance of their precepts: such as they did find, those wise and good men availed themselves of to the utmost, for the benefit of mankind. Virtue they said is agreeable to reason, and therefore ought to be followed by every reasonable being. This is true, and an inducement to those who venerate the law of their own minds; but as that is a law, which every one may dispense with at pleasure, it certainly carries with it no sort of obligation. Temporal inconveniencies, they farther urged, attend the violation of the rules of virtue. This indeed would be a powerful sanction, if things so fell out constantly and invariably: but on the contrary, we see virtue and wickedness promiscuously fortunate and unfortunate in the world. Moral obligation, in short, can arise out of no other principles but these, *viz.* that the laws of virtue are the laws of God; that it

is

is his will, that thofe laws be obeyed by man;
and that we fhall pafs into another ftate, where
every one will be rewarded or punifhed, as he
fhall in this life have obeyed or difobeyed them.
This only fanction of morality, the wifdom,
the penetration, and induftry of the ancients
could not difcover, though they diligently
fought after it.   But that which thefe lights
of the ancient world attempted in vain, what
raw fcholar cannot now perform? What no-
vice, who has a mind to vilify the Chriftian
Revelation as ufelefs to mankind, cannot pre-
fently, by mere dint of reafon, draw out a
complete fyftem of belief, of worfhip, and of
practice? Who cannot now demonftrate the
being, the attributes, and moral government
of God over the World? and conclude, that
being a fpirit, he is to be worfhipped in fpirit
and in truth? Who cannot evince, the laws
of morality to be his laws? bring life and im-
mortality into open day-light? and exhibit
before the eyes of all men that fcene of future
being, wherein every man fhall receive a re-
compence proportioned to his deeds? What
youth I fay, by mere dint of reafon, cannot
now do all this, and much more, at his eafe?
Vile and fhamelefs plagiaries, who having
stolen

stolen their doctrine from the Gospel, and most thievishly disguised it under an altered dress, are not content, when taken in the fact, most impudently to deny the theft, but most ungratefully vilify the author from whom the intire system of their boasted wisdom is most manifestly purloined. But even these great doctrines taken from scripture, were they to be taught in the name only of some reputed wise man, would presently lose their authority, weight and influence, and become, what the ancient philosophy was, mere matter of speculation, of eternal disputing and wrangling, instead of being regarded as obligatory rules of life and manners.

If these things be so; if irreligion be the source of all evil present and future; and if no other experienced, or probable remedy can be suggested proper to subdue it, but propagating the doctrines of revealed religion; then have we great reason to bless God, who put it into the heart of that glorious Prince who had before saved our religion at home from violence, to establish this society for the restoration and revival of it in our colonies abroad, where it was, in many parts, almost expiring through carelessness.

C   An

An evil fo inveterate, and fo widely diffufed, over a vaft tract of country, there could be no hopes of remedying in a fhort time, or with a fmall ftrength. It was plainly feen, that it muft prove a work of many years, of unwearied patience and perfeverance, and would require a collected and well governed force.

For thefe reafons a Corporation to carry on the pious work was eftablifhed, and by a perpetual fucceffion made in fome fenfe immortal. By this advantage of perpetual duration, it is furnifhed with a capacity of carrying on a defign of fo great length to its final accomplifhment. Hence alfo it is enabled to execute its purpofes, not by fits and ftarts, with frequent intermiffions, during which, things naturally of themfelves flide backward, but to proceed with a continued, fteady, uniform endeavour and direction, whereby the moft difficult enterprizes being kept always going forward, are at laft brought to the defired end. Hence alfo it has the advantage of underftanding the beft method of purfuing its ends, by means of a long experience, the beft guide in all human affairs. This Corporation is likewife, as it were, the refervoir of the national charity in this kind; wherein the bounty of each indivi-
dual,

dual, which fingly had been fruitlefs, being collected together, and directed one and the fame way, like the rays of the fun concentered in the fame point, hath wrought much greater effects, than otherwife could have been produced. The integrity of the Society hath ever been not only blamelefs, but free from all fufpicion. In thefe hands therefore every one may with fafety and full confidence intruft his liberality, and reft affured, that by their adminiftration, much more effectually than by his own, the good work he favours, will be carried on and promoted.

Nor let defpondence and defpair of an happy event difcourage the charitable difpofition of any perfon towards this undertaking. The fuccefs of the endeavours hitherto ufed, hath, by the bleffing of God, been confiderable, under many difadvantages; of which fome, even the principal of them, there is ground to hope, will yet one day be removed. The want of feminaries in thofe parts, for the education of perfons to ferve in the miniftry of the Gofpel, is a great difadvantage; fo great, that there is reafon to apprehend, it may one day undo, all that the Society has been fo many years labouring to do. If mini-

nifters

nifters fail, religion muft fail with them: and
can it be imagined that this little fpot of an
ifland can fupply the vaft continent of America, and the iflands of the Weft Indies, daily
increafing by an afflux of new inhabitants?
hath it at any time been able to anfwer the
demands from thence? in the provinces, where
maintenance is by law provided for minifters,
feveral churches have in all times ftood vacant,
becaufe none could be found to officiate in
them. The fame want hath all along been
an hindrance to the proper work of the Society; and muft needs prove an effectual bar
to any farther confiderable progrefs in it. And
may it not be apprehended; (which God
avert!) that from the fame caufe things fooner
or later may begin to go backward. The want
of native minifters looks, in my apprehenfion,
with a malignant afpect on the church there.
Nor is it of late only, that this danger hath
been perceived and dreaded: that glorious
Prince, who eftablifhed this Society, faw and
confidered it; and for remedy thereof, caufed
to be built, and liberally endowed a college in
thofe parts. Unfortunately it hath not anfwered his intention. A fecond feminary for
the fame purpofe hath been raifed by the pious
bounty

bounty of a private gentleman. This too hath failed; and no wonder: for what encouragement have the inhabitants of those regions to qualify themselves for holy orders, while, to obtain them; they lye under the necessity of crossing an immense ocean, with much inconvenience, danger and expence; which those who come hither on that errand can but ill bear? And if they have the fortune to arrive safe, being here without friends, and without acquaintance, they have the sad business to undergo, of presenting themselves unknown, to persons unknown, without any recommendation or introduction, except certain papers in their pocket. Are there not circumstances in this case, sufficient to deter every ordinary courage, and to damp the most adventurous spirit? It hath therefore hitherto proved, and probably will ever be found, a vain expence to build and endow colleges there, while that people have this only method of being admitted to the ministry. Who will qualify themselves? who, on such unjust terms, will seek the office? An office accompanied, there at least, with no tempting advantages, that may counter-balance the above-mentioned discouragements, and hardships. Who would not rather take upon

him

him any other occupation, which he can freely
affume, and exercife without authority and
licence fetched from another hemifphere?
Whoever then wifhes to fee feminaries for
the breeding of minifters flourifh in America,
muft wifh, and, if he hath opportunity, will
endeavour to procure them the means of being
ordained to the miniftry on that fide of the
ocean.

The want then of Bifhops in our colonies,
befides other difadvantages attending it, appears, in particular, to be the fundamental
caufe of the want of native minifters. The
one removed; the other, it feems, would ceafe
of courfe. For can it be imagined, could orders be had on the fame terms there as elfe-
where, that a number of the natives fufficient
for the fervice of the churches, would not
offer themfelves in thofe, as they do,
in all other parts of Chriftendom. But
farther, the want of Bifhops there hath been
all along the more heavily lamented, becaufe
it is a cafe fo fingular, that it cannot be
paralleled in the Chriftian world. For what
fect was ever any where at all allowed, that
was not allowed the means within themfelves of providing for the continual exercife
                                                 of

of their worſhip? the granting one without the other would be but a mockery. Yet ſuch is the ſtate of our church in the colonies; and at a time, and in a realm, where the rights of conſcience are beſt underſtood, and moſt fully allowed and protected. All ſects of Proteſtant Chriſtians here at home; and all, ſave one, throughout our colonies, have the full enjoyment of their religion. Even the Romiſh ſuperſtition, within a province lately added to the Britiſh dominions, is completely allowed in all points; it hath Biſhops and ſeminaries. Thus ſtands the caſe of all churches in our colonies, except only the church here by law eſtabliſhed: that alone is not tolerated in the whole; it exiſts only in part, in a maimed ſtate, lopt of Epiſcopacy, an eſſential part of its conſtitution. And whence this diſgraceful diſtinction? whence this mark of diſtruſt? what is the fear? what the danger? A few perſons veſted with authority to ordain miniſters, to confirm youth, and to viſit their own clergy. Can two or three perſons, reſtrained to theſe ſpiritual functions, be dangerous to any in any matter? in what? or to whom? Can they poſſibly, ſo limited, on any pretence what-

ever

ever, attempt to moleft any in their religious
concerns? Can they invade the rights and
jurifdiction of magiftrates? Can they infringe
the liberties of the people? Can they weaken,
or be thought difpofed to weaken, the fidelity
of the colonies to his Majefty, or their de-
pendence on this country? To thefe duties, if
there be any difference, the members of this
church, as fuch, are bound by one fpecial
motive, befides the many motives common to
them with other fubjects. But if old grudges
and jealoufies be the obftacle; can it be imagined, that obfolete piques, and groundlefs
fears, long fince extinct here, and which
ought there alfo to be extinguifhed, will be
fuffered for ever to prevail againft reafon,
equity and piety?

If thefe things be fo, we may entertain
good hopes, that the difadvantage fo long lamented will fome time be removed; and if
there be no latent mifchief, that will arife to
the ftate from thence; we may affure ourfelves that this benefit will flow to the church
from our prefent moft gracious Sovereign,
whenever public wifdom, public care, public
juftice and piety fhall advife the meafure.
This point obtained, the American church
will

will foon go out of its infant ftate; be able to ftand upon its own legs; and without foreign help fupport and fpread itfelf. Then the bufinefs of this Society will have been brought to the happy iffue intended.

In the mean while, until this happy period arrive, it is of the utmoft importance and neceffity, that the work of the Society be purfued with unwearied patience and zeal. It is a work of the higheft charity, and of the moft extenfive benefit, begun and carried on for the glory of God, for the advancement of Chrift's kingdom, and the falvation of fouls; for delivering multitudes of people from the greateft evils, ignorance of God, and the dominion of fin, with the endlefs train of miferies confequent thereto; and for communicating to them the greateft good, the light of the gofpel, and true righteoufnefs, with the many and perpetual felicities flowing from them. To promote this pious work is a duty bound on every Chriftian, both by the command of Chrift, and the reafon of the thing. It is a duty we owe not only to God, but to our country alfo; whofe peace and profperity effentially depend on the religion and morals of the people. The obli-

D   gations

gations and motives to this duty are very many and very ftrong. Weigh them ferioufly in your minds; confidering withal, that this charitable work hath no other fund to fupply the expences attending it, than the voluntary contributions of good and pious men. Weigh well and confider thefe things deeply in your thoughts; and may Almighty God, whofe providence hath hitherto fupported it, continue to infufe into the hearts of men the fpirit of liberality towards this pious undertaking, until it fhall have accomplifhed its perfect work.

A N

An ABSTRACT of the

CHARTER,

And of the Proceedings of the SOCIETY for the Propagation of the Gospel in Foreign Parts, from the 21ft Day of *February*, 1766, to the 20th Day of *February*, 1767.

KING *William* III. of Glorious Memory, was gracioufly pleafed, on the 16th of *June*, 1701, *to erect and fettle a Corporation with a perpetual Succeffion, by the Name of* THE SOCIETY FOR THE PROPAGATION OF THE GOSPEL IN FOREIGN PARTS; *for the Receiving, Managing, and Difpofing of the Contributions of fuch Perfons as would be induced to extend their Charity towards* the Maintenance of a Learned and an Orthodox Clergy, *and the making fuch other Provifion as might be neceffary for the Propagation of the Gofpel in Foreign Parts, upon Information, that in many of our Plantations, Colonies, and Factories beyond the Seas, the Provifion for Minifters was mean, and many other of our faid Plantations, Colonies, and Factories, were wholly unprovided of a Maintenance for Minifters, and the publick Worfhip of God; and that, for lack of Support and Maintenance*

D 2 *of*

of ſuch, many of his loving Subjects wanted the Adminiſtration of God's Word and Sacraments, and ſeemed to be abandoned to Atheiſm and Infidelity, and others of them to Popiſh Superſtition and Idolatry.

The Society was compoſed, by the Charter, of the Chief Prelates and Dignitaries of the Church, and of ſeveral other Lords, and eminent Perſons in the State, with a Power to elect ſuch others to be Members of the Corporation, as they, or the major Part of them, ſhould think beneficial to their charitable Deſigns; and they immediately applied themſelves with great Zeal and Alacrity to the good Work; and after adjuſting Preliminaries in the Choice of Officers, and ſettling ſtanding. Orders and Rules for their more regular Proceeding, they ſubſcribed every one of them according to their ſeveral Ranks and Diſpoſitions, an annual Sum to be paid to their Treaſurer, for the general Uſes of the Society; and choſe new Members, and gave out Deputations according to the Powers in the Charter, to receive and collect the Donations of all charitable and well-diſpoſed Perſons towards this moſt pious Deſign : And thro' an eſpecial Bleſſing, *this Work of the Lord hath* hitherto *proſpered in their Hands.* Many more than One Hundred and Forty Thouſand of our own People, Infants and Adults, and many Thouſands of *Indians* and *Negroes,* have been inſtructed and baptized into the true Faith of our Lord Jeſus Chriſt; and more than One Hundred

Hundred and Fifty Thoufand Volumes of Bibles and Common Prayer Books, with other Books of Devotion and Inftruction, together with an innumerable Quantity of pious fmall Tracts, have been difperfed in Foreign Parts; and there is now a very hopeful and improving Appearance of Religion in the public Worſhip of God, according to the Liturgy of the Church of *England,* in a great number of Churches in our Plantations in *America,* by the Means, and through the Procurement, of this Corporation.

The Charter directs the Society to give an Annual Account to the Lord High Chancellor, the Lord Chief Juftice of the *King's Bench,* and the Lord Chief Juftice of the *Common Pleas,* of the feveral Sums of Money by them received, and laid out, and of the Management and Difpofition of the Revenues of the Corporation: This is punctually done, and the Society annually make public an Abftract of them and their Proceedings. Therefore the Society now, in the firft Place, acknowledge the Receipt, and return their moft hearty Thanks for the particular Benefactions of the Year 1766, *viz.*

	l.	*s.*	*d.*
To a Lady unknown, by *Calverly Bewicke,* Efq; for -	1	1	0
To Mrs. *Lucy Osborne* ——	2	2	0
To the Rev. Mr. *Benj. Archer,* Rector of *Stour Provoſt, Dorſetſhire,* —	2	2	0

To

	£	s.	d.
To a Lady, desiring to be unknown, by his Grace the Lord Archbishop of *Canterbury*, — —	5	8	0
To the Rev. Sir *Ashurst Allin*, Bart. of *Lowestoffe*, *Suffolk*, a Collection from his Parish, — —	2	11	0
To *P. T.* ——— ———	10	0	0
To Mrs. *Kelsey*, by Mr. *Cotton*, —	1	1	0
To Mrs. *Catherine Kelsey*, by ditto, —	1	1	0
To Mrs. *Parker*, by ditto, ——	1	1	0
To Mrs. *Pearce*, by ditto, ——	2	2	0
To Mrs. *Eliz. Torriano*, her Subscription to *Christmas*, 1765, —	5	5	0
For a further Part of the Rev. Mr. *Henderson*'s Legacy, by Mr. *Tyler*, Executor,	50	0	0
To *P. E.* —— ——	4	4	0
To the Dean of *York*, and his Friends,	28	12	0
To a Lady unknown, by the Rev. Dr. *Lloyd*, Dean of *Norwich*, —	80	0	0
To another Lady unknown, by ditto,	2	2	0
To *A. P.* a Bank Note, ——	10	0	0
To *Charles Jennens*, Esq; of *Gopsal* in *Leicestershire*, by Mr. *Hetherington*,	21	0	0
To Mrs. *Eliz. Hanmer*, by ditto, —	5	5	0
To a *London* Clergyman unknown, by the Rev. Mr. *Broughton*, —	1	1	0
For the Legacy of Mrs. *Eliz. Byerley*, by Mr. *Thomas Hill*, one of her Executors, —— ——	3000	0	0
To Miss *Palmer*, an annual Subscription,	2	2	0
To Mrs. *Elwes*, of *Chiswick*, ——	100	0	0
To a Lady unknown, by Mrs. *Lane*,	10	10	0

To

To a Lady unknown, by Mr. *Pearce*,	15	0	0
To *Henry Southby*, Efq; of *Caverfham*, *Oxfordfhire*,	1	1	0
To Mr. *Tyrrell*, of *Ormond Street*, by the Rev. Dr. *Plumptree*,	10	0	0
To Mifs *Cordelia Bright*, her Subfcription to. *Chriftmas*, 1765,	3	3	0
To *Thomas Barker*, Efq; of *Lindon*, *Rutlandfhire*, by the Rev. Mr. *Wilfon*, of *Empingham*,	2	2	0
To Mrs. *Barker*, jun. by ditto,	0	10	6
To Mrs. *Margaret Floyer*, of *Dorchefter*, by Mr. *Robert Lewis*,	10	0	0
For the Legacy of the Rev. Mr. *Thomas Winder*, for propagating the Gofpel where it has not yet been preached, by his Executors,	100	0	0
To Mrs. *Parkhurft*, Widow,	50	0	0
For the Refidue of Mr. *David Brevett*'s Legacy of 100 *l*.	50	0	0
To Mrs. *Sufanna Mathew*, by Mr. *Gregfon*,	1	1	0
For the Legacy of Sir *John Philipps*, by Lady *Philipps*, his Executrix,	50	0	0
For Intereft of ditto,	2	0	0
For the Legacy of *Richard Newman*, Efq; by his Executors,	100	0	0
To Mrs. *Dennis*,	10	10	0
To a Lady unknown, by the Rev. Dr. *Hallifax*,	1	1	0
For the Legacy of the Rev. Mr. *Purnell*, of *Manchefter*, by his Executors,	30	0	0

To

To a Person unknown, by Mr. *Staples*,	20	0	0
To the Rev. Mr. *Hughes*, ——	1	1	0
To Mrs. *Ann Maynard,* by Messrs. *Hoare* and Co. ——	10	10	0
For the Legacy of Mrs. *Eliz. Ludwell,* by *Francis Austen*, Esq; ——	500	0	0
To a Person unknown, by *John Palairet*, Esq; —— ——	30	0	0
For the Legacy of the Rev. Mr. *Francis Drake*, by Mr. *James Drake*, Executor,	20	0	0
For the Legacy of *Robert North*, Esq; by the Rev. Mr. *Thomas Adams*,	250	0	0
For the Legacy of Mr. *Edward Hemming*, in New *South Sea* Annuities, transferred to the Society by his Executors, —— ——	300	0	0
For half a Year's Dividend on the said Legacy, due *July* 5, ——	4	10	0
For the Legacy of Mrs. *Hannah Catlen*, by Mr. *Thomas Vialls*, Executor,	150	0	0
For the Legacy of Mrs. *Margaret Hunt*, by *Edward Yardley*, Esq; Executor,	500	0	0
To Mrs. *Elwes*, of *Chiswick*, by Mr. *Walter Dicker*, ——	100	0	0
To the Rev. Sir *Ashurst Allin*, Bart. of *Somerly Hall*, *Suffolk*, a Collection from his Parish, ——	2	11	0
For the Residue of *Sarah Complin*'s Legacy, —— ——	0	5	0
For the Legacy of Mrs. *Kelsey*, by her Executrixes, ——	5	5	0

To

To *Roger Pratt*, of *Riston* in *Norfolk*, Esq; by the Rev. Dr. *Stedman*,	5	5	0
To a Gentlewoman unknown, by the Rev. Dr. *Tew*,	1	1	0
To the Rev. Mr. Archdeacon *Sharpe*,	1	1	0
To a Lady unknown, by Mr. *Venn*,	50	0	0
To Miss *Sydenham*, her annual Conrribution,	4	4	0
To the Rev. Dr. *Tew*, Rector of *Boldon* near *Newcastle*, by *Robert Markland*, Esq;	100	0	0
To a Gentleman of *Lowth*, in *Lincolnshire*, by his Friend in *London*,	2	2	0
To Mr. *Elias Brown*, by Mr. *William Yeathard*,	2	2	0
To Mrs. *Vic*, of *Clifton*, near *Bristol*, by the Rev. Dr. *Tucker*, Dean of *Glocester*,	5	5	0
To Mrs. *Toogood*, of *Bristol*, by ditto,	1	1	0
To Mrs. *S. P.* by ditto,	1	1	0
To a Person desiring to be unknown, by ditto,	4	4	0
To a Person unknown, by Mr. Archdeacon *Head*,	2	2	0
To the Rev. Mr. *Priest*, by the Rev. Mr. *Broughton*,	1	1	0
To the Rev. Mr. *Fenwicke*, of *Hallaton* near *Harborough*,	1	1	0
To Mrs. *Bewicke*, by ditto,	3	0	0
To Mrs. *Sarah Carte*, by ditto,	1	1	0
To *J. E. W.*	6	6	0
To a Person unknown, by *John Palairet*, Esq;	30	0	0

E To

To the Rev. Mr. *Harvey*, of *Lowshill*, *Suffolk*,	2	2	0
To the Subdean of *Exeter*,	8	8	0
To the Hon. Mrs. *Shirley*,	5	5	0
To *Humphrey Fitzherbert*, of *Bristol*, Esq;	2	2	0
To Mrs. *Elizabeth Torriano*,	5	5	0
For the Legacy of the Rev. Mr. *Hilary*, by *Joseph Allen*, M. D.	50	0	0
To a Person unknown, remitted by the Rev. Mr. *Taylor*, Minister of *Clifton*, near *Bristol*,	5	5	0
To the Rev. Dr. *Knail*, Vicar of *Carisbrook*, in the *Isle of Wight*,	1	1	0
To Sir *John Oglander*, by ditto,	1	1	0
To Mr. *John Oglander*, by ditto,	1	1	0
To Mrs. *Leigh*, of *Northcot*, by ditto,	1	1	0
To the Rev. Dr. *Walker*, of *Molleston*, by ditto,	1	1	0
To *David Urry*, Esq; by ditto,	1	1	0
To the Rev. Mr. *Culme*, Rector of *Freshwater*, by ditto,	1	1	0
To the Rev. Mr. *Walter*, Rector of *Brixtone*, by ditto,	1	1	0
To the Rev. Mr. *Troughear Holmes*, by ditto,	1	1	0
To Mr. *Leigh*, of *Thorley*, by ditto,	0	10	6
To *William White*, Esq; by ditto,	0	10	6
To *Robert Worsley*, Esq; by ditto,	0	10	6
To Mr. *Clark*, of *Newport*, by ditto,	0	10	6
To *Robert Pope Blachford*, Esq; by ditto,	1	1	0
To a Member of the Society, desiring to be unknown,	3	3	0
To the Rev. Mr. *Marrian Feaver*, of *Dorsetshire*,	1	1	0

To:

To Lady *Ann Shadwell,* ——	1	11	6
To *R. B.* —— ——	5	5	0
To Lady *Curzon,* —— ——	5	5	0
To a Clergyman in the Eaft of *Suffex,* } ·by·the· Rev. Mr. *Edward Wilfon,*	1	1	0

Thefe Benefactions, together with Ten Pounds, Ten Shillings, paid at Entrance of new Members, amounting to the Sum of Six Thoufand and Nineteen Pounds, Thirteen Shillings, are all the Benefactions to the Society in the Year 1766; of which the Sum of Four Thoufand Nine Hundred and Thirty Pounds, Fourteen Shillings and Five Pence, has been expended in Salaries, and other incidental Charges, and for Books fent by the Society to *North America,* and the Society have been encouraged to erect feveral new Miffions, and employ more School-mafters.

The Names of the Society's Missionaries, together with those of the Society's Catechists and School-masters, with their respective Salaries, are as follow :

Newfoundland.

Annual.
Salaries.

£.

1 Mr. *Langman*, Missionary at St. *John's* Town, — — } 50
2 Mr. *Balfour*, Missionary at *Trinity Bay*,   50
3 Mr. *Coughlan*, Missionary at *Harbour Grace* and *Carboneer*, — } 50

Nova Scotia.

4 Mr. *Wood*, Missionary at *Annapolis Royal*, and *Grandville*, — } 70
5 Mr. *Wilkie*, School-master at *Annapolis*,   10
6 Mr. *Morison*, School-master at *Grandville*, 10
7 Mr. *Breynton*, Missionary at *Halifax*,   70
8 Mr, *Lynch*, School-master at *Halifax*,   10
9 Mr. *Moreau*, Missionary to the *French* at *Lunenburgh*, — — } 70
10 Mr. *Bailly*, School-master to the *French* at *Lunenburgh*, — } 15
11 Mr. *Bryzelius*, Missionary at *Lunenburgh*, 70
12 Mr. *Neuman*, Assistant School-master at *Lunenburgh*, — } 10
13 Mr. *Joseph Bennet*, Missionary at *Horton*, *Windsor*, *Newport*, and *Cornwallis*, } 70

14

14 Mr.   School-master for *Horton* and
     Cornwallis, ———   ——— } 10

15 Mr.   School-master for *Windsor* and
     Newport, ———   } 10

New England.

Province of New Hampshire.

16 Mr *Arthur Browne,* Missionary at *Ports-*
     mouth, ——— ——   —— } 60

——— ——— for officiating at *Kittery,* ——— 15

17 Mr. *Badger,* Itinerant Missionary in *New*
     Hampshire, ———   — } 50

Province of Massachusets Bay.

18 Mr. *Bailey,* Itinerant Missionary on the
     Eastern Frontiers, ——   — } 50

19 Mr.   Missionary at *George Town,*
     and Places adjacent, on *Kennebeck*
     River, ———   —— } 30

20 Mr. *Wiswall,* Missionary at *Falmouth* in
     Casco Bay, ——   —— } 20

21 Mr. *Bass,* Missionary at *Newbury,* —— 50

22 Mr. *Wecks,* Missionary at *Marblehead,* 50

23 Mr. *Macgilchrist,* Missionary at *Salem,* 50

24 Mr. *Sergeant,* Missionary at *Cambridge,* 50

25 Mr. *Winslow,* Missionary at *Braintree,*
     Stoughton, and *Dedham,* —— } 60

26 Mr. *Ebenezer Thompson,* Missionary at
     Scituate, and *Marshfield,* —— } 50

Colony

Colony of Rhode Island.

27 Mr. *Marmaduke Browne*, Missionary at Newport, — — } 50

28 Mr. *Fayerweather*, Missionary at *Naraganset*, — — — } 50

29 Mr. *Usher*, Missionary at *Bristol*, — 60

30 Mr. *John Graves*, Missionary at *Providence*, — — } 50

———— for officiating at *Warwick*, — 15

31 Mr. *Taylor*, School-master at *Providence*, 10

Colony of Connecticut.

32 Dr. *Johnson*, Missionary at *Stratford*, 50

33 Mr. *Newton*, Missionary at *Ripton*, 30

34 Mr. *Lamson*, Missionary at *Fairfield*, 50

35 Mr. *Dibblee*, Missionary at *Stamford*, 50

36 Mr. *Mathew Graves*, Missionary at *New London*, — — } 60

37 Mr.   School-master to the *Naraganset Indians*, — } 15

38 Mr. *Beach*, Missionary at *Newtown* and *Reading*, — } 50

39 Mr. *Clarke*, Missionary at *New Haven* and *West Haven*, — } 40

40 Mr. *Gibbs*, Missionary at *Simsbury* and *Hartland*, — } 30

41 Mr. *Viets*, Assistant to Mr. *Gibbs*, 20

42 Mr. *Mansfield*, Missionary at *Derby* and *Oxford*, — — } 40

43 Mr. *Leaming*, Missionary at *Norwalk*, 50

44

44 Mr.   Miffionary at *New Mil-*
   ford, Woodbury, Kent, and *New Fair-* } 30
   field,   ———   ——

45 Mr. *Palmer,* Miffionary at *Litchfield,* }
   Cornwall, Sharon, and *Great Bar-* } 30
   rington,   ———   ——

46 Mr. *Scovil,* Miffionary at *Waterbury,* }
   Weftbury, Northbury, and *New Cam-* } 30
   bridge,   ——   ——

47 Mr. *Peters,* Miffionary at *Hebron,*   30

48 Mr. *Andrews,* Miffionary at *Walling-* }
   ford, Chefhire, Meridan, and *North* } 20
   Haven,   ——   ——

49 Mr.   Miffionary at *Norwich,*   30

New York.

50 Mr. *Cutting,* Miffionary at *Hempftead* }
   on *Long Ifland,*   ——   —— } 30

51 Mr. *Avery,* Miffionary at *Rye,*   ——   40

52 Mr. *Wetmore,* School-mafter at *Rye,*   10

53 Mr. *Charlton,* Miffionary at *Staten* }
   Ifland,   ——   —— } 50

54 Mr. *Egberts,* School-mafter at *Staten* }
   Ifland,   ——   —— } 15

55 Mr. *Samuel Seabury,* Miffionary at *Eaft* }
   and *Weft Chefter,*   —— } 40

5 Mr. *Nathaniel Seabury,* School-mafter }
   at *Weft Chefter,*   ——   —— } 10

57 Mr. *Munro,* Miffionary at *Philipfburg,*   30

58 Mr.   Miffionary at *Schenec-* }
   tady,   ———   —— } 30

59

59 Mr. *Thomas Brown*, Missionary at *Al-*
    bany, and to the *Mohawk Indians*,   } 50

60 Mr.   Catechist to the
    Mohawk Indians, ——   } 40

61 Mr. *Oël*, Assistant in instructing the
    Indians,   ——   —— } 10

62 *Paulus*, a *Mohawk*, School-master to
    the *Indians*,   ——   } 7 10

63 Mr.   Missionary at *Newburgh*,   30

64 Mr. *Hildreth*, School-master at *New*
    York,   ——   —— } 15

65 Mr. *Beardsley*, Missionary at *Pogh-*
    keepsie, in *Dutches* County, } 30

New Jersey.

66 Dr. *Chandler*, Missionary at *Elizabeth*
    Town,   ——   —— } 50

67 Mr. *Mackean*, Missionary at *Amboy*
    and *Woodbridge*,   —— } 50

68 Mr. *Odell*, Missionary at *Burlington*,   50

69 Mr. *Evans*, Missionary at *Glocester* and
    Waterford,   ——   } 40

70 Mr. *Cooke*, Missionary in *Monmouth*
    County,   ——   —— } 60

71 Mr. *Isaac Browne*, Missionary at
    Newark,   ——   —— } 50

72 Mr.   Missionary at *New*
    Brunswick and *Piscataqua*, } 40

73 Mr. *Dow*, School-master at *Second*
    River,   ——   —— } 10

74 Mr. *Spencer*, Miffionary at St. *Peter's* Spotf*wood*, and St. *Peter's Freehold*, } 35

75 Mr. _____ Miffionary at *Trenton* and *Maidenhead*, — —— } 50

Pennfylvania.

76 Mr. *Rofs*, Miffionary at *Newcaftle*, — 60
77 Mr. *Reading*, Miffionary at *Apoquinimink*, 60
78 Mr. *Craig*, Miffionary at *Chefter*, 60
79 Mr. _____ Miffionary at *Oxford*, 60
80 Mr. *Currie*, Miffionary at *Radnor*, 60
81 Mr. *Magaw*, Miffionary at *Dover* and *Duck Creek*, — —— } 40
82 Mr. _____ Miffionary at *Mifpillion*, St. *Paul's* near *Maryland*, and *Cedar Creek*, } 40
83 Mr. *John Andrews*, Miffionary at *Lewes* in *Suffex County*, —— } 40
84 Mr. *Barton*, Itinerant Miffionary in *Lancafter*, —— —— } 50
85 Mr. *William Thomfon*, Itinerant Miffionary in the Counties of *York* and *Cumberland*, —— — } 50
86 Mr. *Murray*, Miffionary at *Reading*, 30

North Carolina.

87 Mr. *Earl*, Miffionary at St. *Paul's* Parifh, *Chowan County*, —— } 50
88 Mr. *Stewart*, Miffionary at St. *Thomas's*, *Bath Town*, —— —— } 50
89 Mr. *Reed*, Miffionary in *Craven County*, 50

F

90

90 Mr. *Thomlinfon*, School-mafter at *New-bern*, } 15

91 Mr. *Barnet*, Miffionary at *Brunfwick*, 50

92 Mr. *Micklejohn*, Miffionary in *Rowan County*, } 20

93 Mr. *Morton*, Miffionary in *Northampton County*, } 20

Georgia.

94 Mr. *Zouberbuhler*, Miffionary at *Savannah*, 50
95 Mr. *Frink*, Miffionary at *Augufta*, — 50
96 Mr. *Alexander*, Miffionary at *St. John's*, 30

Bahama Iflands.

97 Mr. *Tizard*, Miffionary at *New Provi-dence*, } 60

98 Mr. *Bafcome*, School-mafter at *New Pro-vidence*, } 10

99 Mr. *Mofs*, Miffionary at *Harbour Ifland* and *Eleuthera*, } 60

100 Mr. School-mafter at *Harbour Ifland*, } 10

Africa.

101 Mr. *Philip Quaque*, Miffionary, Cate-chift, and School-mafter to the *Negroes* on the Gold Coaft, } 50

Total £ 3997 10 0

Barbadoes.

Barbadoes.

102 Mr. *Butcher*, School-mafter at *Co-* ⎫
    drington College, ——— ⎬ 100
103 Mr. *Wharton*, Affiftant in the School, ⎫
    and Catechift to the *Negroes* — ⎬ 70
104 Mr. *Bowen*, for teaching Writing ⎫
    and Arithmetick, — ⎬ 40

N. B. Thefe Salaries are paid out of the Produce of the Plantation.

The Society allow Ten Pounds Worth of Books to each Miffion for a Library, and Five Pounds Worth of pious fmall Tracts to every new Miffionary, to be diftributed among his Parifhioners, and other Parcels of Books, as Occafion offers, and the Society find them wanting. And the Society have received the following Accounts of their pious Labours in the Year 1766.

Newfoundland.

By a Letter from the Rev. Mr. *Langman*, the Society's Miffionary at *St. John's*, dated *Nov.* 8, 1766, it appears, that upon the laft Survey, there were in this Place (exclufive of the Garrifon) 241 *Englifh* Men, 78 Women, and 158 Children; 477 *Irifh* Men, 65 Women, and 113 Children; in the whole 1132 Souls. In the Courfe of the Year he baptized 47 Infants, buried 35 Corpfes, and married 14 Couple, and has about 24 Communicants.

The

The Rev. Mr. *Balfour*, the Society's Miſſionary at *Trinity Bay*, in his Letter dated *November* 17, 1766, writes, that in *Trinity Bay*
are 320 Men, who are Proteſtants, 416 Roman
Catholics, and 196 Women and Children; that
he baptized within the Year 30, buried 25, and
had 9 Communicants, who have an Opportunity of receiving the holy Communion the firſt
Sunday of every Month in the Summer Seaſon.
In ſeaſonable Weather he teaches *gratis* a few
Children who attend him in his own Houſe at
leiſure Hours, and ſuch as are capable repeat
the Catechiſm in Church.

Upon the Petition of the Inhabitants of *Harbour Grace* and *Carboneer*, the Society have this
Year appointed another Miſſionary in thoſe Parts,
the Rev. Mr. *Lawrence Coughlan*, a Gentleman
recommended by the Inhabitants, among whom
he had reſided ſome Time as their Miniſter, and
to whoſe ſupport they promiſe to contribute to
the utmoſt of their Abilities.

Nova Scotia.

The Society have received this Year from
Jonathan Belcher, Eſq; Preſident of the Council
and Chief Juſtice of *Nova Scotia*, two Letters
dated *Jan.* 27, and *Oct.* 7, 1766, lamenting the
Loſs the Province has ſuſtained by the Death of
ſo able and prudent a Miniſter as Mr. *Vincent*,
and expreſſing his Opinion of the Neceſſity of
appointing a Miſſionary at *Lunenburg*, qualified
to

to officiate in *German* as well as *English.* He speaks highly of Mr. *Bennet's* Labours, who in the Service of four Townships has been employed without the leaft Abatement of Zeal and good Conduct. At the Defire of Mr. *Belcher* and feveral other Gentlemen, the Society have appointed Mr. *Lynch* School-mafter at *Halifax*, where they have lately paffed an Act of Affembly for the better Regulation of Schools and Schoolmafters throughout the Province.

The Society have received this Year four Letters from the Rev. Mr. *Wood*, Miffionary at *Annapolis Royal* and *Granville*, dated *Oct.* 15, 1765, *May* 31, *July* 27, and *Sept.* 4, 1766, in which he writes, that it is not poffible to afcertain the Number of Indians in this Province, as they feldom ftay a Month in a Place. Some of them fpeak *French*, a few *English*, but moft of them know no other Language but *Mickmack*, which Mr. *Wood* is ftudying very clofely. He flatters himfelf, that the Religious Principles the *Indians* have imbibed from the *French* Priefts will wear off, if no more Romifh Priefts be fettled among them. He writes, that Mr. *Wilkie*, the Society's School-mafter at *Annapolis*, goes on well, and has between 40 and 50 Scholars, and about 20 of them are catechized publickly every *Sunday*; and that Mr. *Morrifon*, licenfed School-mafter at *Granville*, whom the Society have taken into their Service, is a fober, difcreet young Man, and likely to be very ufeful in his Station. Mr. *Wood* has fent this Year the Lord's

Prayer

Prayer and the Apostle's Creed, in the *Mickmack* Language, together with a *French* and *English* Copy of the first Part of his *Mickmack* Grammar.

The Rev. Mr. *Breynton*, the Society's Missionary at *Halifax*, in his Letters dated *Oct.* 11, 1765, and *Sept* 4, 1766, recommends the Appointment of a Missionary at *Lunenburg*, qualified to officiate in *German* as well as *English*, by which means 1200 *Germans*, already settled there will be kept united Members of the Church of England, and some thousands who are daily expected will have the Benefit of hearing the Word of God in their own Language, till the rising Generation shall become *English*. And the Society have the Pleasure to inform the Publick, that the Rev. Mr. *Bryselius*, qualified to officiate in both Languages, is now appointed to the Mission of *Lunenburg*, in the room of Mr. *Vincent*. Mr. *Breynton's* Mission continues in its usual prosperous State, Benevolence and mutual Forbearance prevailing among all Persuasions. By his *Notitia Parochialis* it appears, that the Number of Professors of the Church of *England* in and about *Halifax*, including *Germans*, *French*, and *Irish*, is 950, of the Navy 700, of the Army 500, of Protestant Dissenters 350, of constant Communicants 90, of *French* and *German* Communicants 60, of Births within the Year 140, of Burials 50.

The Rev. Mr. *Morcau*, the Society's Missionary to the *French* at *Lunenburg*, in his Letters,

ters, dated *April* 5, and *Sept.* 29 1765, obferves, that all the *Germans*, except a few old People, appear difpofed to join with the Church of *England*, efpecially if fupplied with a Miffionary able to preach in *German* and *Englifh*. At *Whitfuntide* he adminiftered the holy Communion to above 100 Perfons, *Englifh*, *Germans* and *French*, to each in their own Language; among whom were fome young People, who were admitted after a long private Examination in the principal Articles of our holy Religion. His Congregation, he fays, behaves with great Decency and Devotion, and increafes by Marriages fo much that he hopes to fee it foon one of the moft flourifhing on the Continent, as well as remarkably diftinguifhed by its inviolable Attachment to the Principles of the Church of *England*, and by true Holinefs. The *Indians* (for whom Mr. *Moreau* has lately baptized 12 Children, and married one Couple) have fhewn him the Copy of a Letter, which they are told was written by *Jefus Chrift*, to the Bifhop of *Luçon* in *France*, to be fent to them. It is figned by two Perfons, who fay they have received it from the faid Bifhop to be diftributed among the Savages. Each of them have a Copy of it, which they wear next their Heart. The Letter is filled with the groffeft Abfurdities imaginable. They are therein threatened with eternal Damnation, if they fail in any Point of the Romifh Religion; and on the contrary, are promifed endlefs Happinefs, if they feparate from thofe of a different Opinion.

Opinion. They are never to die a sudden Death, nor be drowned, nor perish in War, so long as they have this Letter next their Heart. Mr. *Moreau* is promised leave to take a Copy of this Letter, which he will not fail to transmit to the Society. In the last Year he baptized 80 Children, *English*, *German* and *French*, and married 20 Couple. He assures the Society, that Mr. *Bailly*, School-master to the *French* at *Lunenburg*, is a very pious, modest, sober Man, and very prudent and diligent in the Discharge of his Duty.

The Rev. Mr. *Bennet*, the Society's Missionary at *Horton*, *Windsor*, *Newport*, and *Cornwallis*, in his Letter dated *Jan.* 27, 1766, acquaints the Society, that notwithstanding the Arrival of a Dissenting Minister at *Cornwallis*, a Spirit of Benevolence and Harmony is kept up among People of all Persuasions, who assemble together for Publick Worship. Since his last of *June* 24, 1765, he has baptized 20 Children, and 4 Adults of one Family in *Cornwallis*, who are since admitted into the Number of his Communicants, which is now increased to 30.

New England.

The Rev. Mr. *Arthur Browne*, the Society's Missionary at *Portsmouth* in *New Hampshire*, in his Letter dated *May* 24, 1766, recommends Mr. *Moses Badger*, a Native of *New England*, educated at *Harvard* College, as a suitable Person
son

fon for the Itinerant Miffion in *New Hampfhire,* being well acquainted with the Manners and Cuftoms of the People he is defigned to officiate among, and very acceptable to them. The Eftablifhment of this Miffion, it is hoped, will prove a happy Event to great Numbers of People fcattered up and down in the newly fettled Townfhips in this Government, and be a Means of fecuring fome of thofe many valuable Grants made to the Society by Governor *Wentworth.* Mr. *Browne*'s own Parifhioners are at Peace among themfelves; but the Quiet of the Town, he fays, is greatly interrupted by one *Sandeman,* whofe Scheme is to explode the Ufefulnefs of Prayer and Preaching, and to damn all Oppofers. Of this Gentleman another Miffionary writes, that he feems filled with Bitternefs againft all eftablifhed Churches, and is generally fufpected to be no Friend to the Proteftant Intereft. And another complaining of the pernicious Tendency of Mr. *Sandeman*'s Preaching, fays, that it feems defigned to propagate Infidelity and Libertinifm under a Notion of free Grace; and that the Sum of his Doctrine is, that Chrift has done all and every thing for our Salvation, which God requires of us; that the mere Belief or Affent to this Report is faving Faith, and to have the leaft Solicitude about any Thing, which we have to do in order to obtain Salvation, is the damning Sin of Unbelief, in which all the Chriftian World, except his Sect, is involved.

G The

The Rev. Mr. *Bailey*, the Society's Itinerant Miffionary on the Eaftern Frontiers of *Maffachu-lets Bay*, in his Letters dated *Sept.* 29, 1765, *Sept.* 23, and *Nov.* 18, 1766, returns Thanks, in the Name of the Church People at *George Town* and Places adjacent on *Kennebeck* River, for the Society's kind Intention of fupplying them with a Miffionary, to whofe Support they will readily contribute. The Society have given leave to Mr. *Wheeler*, recommended by Mr. *Bailey* and the People of *George Town*, to come over for holy Orders, to be appointed to this new Miffion, if found worthy. Mr. *Bailey* writes, that a great Number of *Indians* frequent this Neighbourhood. They are the Remains of the ancient *Norridgewalk* Tribe, and lead a rambling Life : They fupport themfelves entirely by hunting, are very favage in their Drefs and Manners, have a Language of their own, but univerfally fpeak *French*, and all profefs the Romifh Religion, and vifit *Canada* once or twice a Year for Abfolution. They have a great Averfion to the *Englifh* Nation, chiefly owing to the Influence of Roman Catholic Miffionaries, who, inftead of endeavouring to reform their Morals, comply with them in their moft extravagant Vices, and teach them that nothing is neceffary to eternal Salvation, but to believe in the Name of *Chrift*, to acknowledge the Pope his holy Vicar, and to extirpate the *Englifh*, becaufe they cruelly murdered the Saviour of Mankind. He concludes one of his Letters with a Detail of the great

great Things Dr. *Gardner*, a Phyfician at *Bofton*, has done and is doing for the Church of *England* in thefe Parts; particularly, his generoufly giving the People of *Pownalborough*, the Ufe of *Richmond* Houfe and Farm feven Years, for Mr. *Bailey*'s Improvement; his fubfcribing largely, and foliciting a Subfcription for building them a Church and Parfonage Houfe; his publifhing at his own Expence an Edition of Bifhop *Beveridge*'s Sermon on the Excellency of the Common Prayer, which has been difperfed to good Purpofe; his Intention to give a Glebe, build a Church and Parfonage Houfe, and endow it for the Support of an Epifcopal Minifter at *Gardner*'s Town. From *Sept.* 26, 1764, to *Sept.* 29, 1765, he baptized 43 Infants and 3 Adults; and from *Sept.* 29, 1765, to *Sept.* 23, 1766, baptized 38 Infants and 1 Adult; and in each Year had an Addition of 2 new Communicants.

The Rev. Mr. *Wifwal*, the Society's Miffionary at *Falmouth* in *Cafco Bay*, in the Province of *Maffachufets*, in his Letters dated *Sept.* 11, 1765, and *July* 25, 1766, acquaints the Society, that fince his Arrival at this new Miffion in *May* 1765, his Congregation is increafed to 70 Families, who conftantly attend publick Worfhip, together with a confiderable Number of Strangers. From *May* 1765 to *July* 1766, he baptized 1 Adult and 27 Children, 2 of them Blacks, and has 21 conftant Communicants. Befides reading Prayers and preaching on the principal Feftivals, and twice every *Sunday*, he adminifters the Sacrament of the

G 2   Lord's

Lord's Supper the first *Sunday* in every Month,
from *Easter* to *Christmas*, and catechises the Children the *Wednesday* following every Sacrament
Day, encouraging those who make the greatest
Proficiency, by presenting each of them with a
Bible or Prayer Book. He promises to visit the
neighbouring Settlements as often as he can.

The Rev. Mr. *Marmaduke Browne*, the Society's Missionary at *Newport* in *Rhode Island*, in
his Letters dated *Jan.* 2 and *July* 1, 1766, writes,
that he is constantly engaged in a Succession of
parochial Duty, as much as he is well able to
struggle with, and has the Comfort to observe,
that much Good is done here, notwithstanding
many Disadvantages they labour under in this
Colony. Within the Year he baptized 43 Infants, 2 white and 1 black Adult, and has 120
Communicants, 7 of whom are Blacks, who
behave in a Manner truly exemplary and praiseworthy.

The Rev. Mr. *Dibblee*, the Society's Missionary at *Stamford* in *Connecticut*, in his Letters
dated *Oct.* 28, 1765, *Mar.* 25, and *Oct.* 7, 1766,
expresses his Satisfaction in the religious Behaviour of his People, which is a great Encouragement to him in the Discharge of the Duty of his
extensive Mission. *Sunday Aug.* 25, 1765, he attended divine Service in the new Church in the
upper District of *Salem*, and preached to a numerous Congregation, had upwards of 30 Communicants, and baptized 13 Children. The like he
did in *August*, 1766, when he had about the same
Number

Number of Communicants, and baptized 15 Children. He has occasionally performed divine Service in this Place for 15 or 16 Years, in pure Compaſſion to the deſtitute Circumſtances of this People, and the People of the adjacent Places, who ſtand in great Need of proper Inſtruction. At the Requeſt of Mr. *St. George Talbot*, he preached at the Opening of a new Church at *Danbury*, 30 Miles diſtant, which, through Mr. *Talbot's* Aſſiſtance, is covered and incloſed, and has a handſome Steeple. A good Congregation gave devout Attendance, among whom were many Diſſenters. The next Day he preached in the private Houſe of a ſober zealous Diſſenter, five Miles from *Danbury*, where a greater Number than was expected attended the Service, and behaved devoutly. Some time after he preached in the Church of *North Caſtle* to a good Congregation, and baptized ſeveral Children. He has lately had an Acceſſion of ſundry Heads of Families to his Pariſh, whoſe Chriſtian Deportment, he doubts not, will do Honour to their Profeſſion. In the Year and half preceding the Date of his laſt Letter, he baptized 119 Children and 12 Adults, and had 8 new Communicants.

The Rev. Mr. *Matthew Graves*, the Society's Miſſionary at *New London* in *Connecticut*, in his Letter dated *June* 3, 1765 (received not till the Year 1766) earneſtly recommends to the Care of the Society, the *Narraganſet Indians*, who requeſt that a School-maſter may be provided

vided for them in the room of Mr. *Cornelius Bennet*. The generous Donation of 40 Acres of Land, which these *Indians* have given towards a Church, their Progress in Religion, their Love to ours in particular, and their steady Adherence to the Crown of *England* from the very first, Mr. *Graves* hopes will engage the Society to supply them with a proper School-master, whom he will readily undertake to oversee and direct, and will visit these *Indians* as often as he can, as he finds them very desirous of religious Instruction, and worthy of Encouragement. The Board immediately complied with this Request, and desired Mr. *Graves* to procure a proper Person to be School-master to the *Narraganset Indians*. This Mr. *Graves*, in his Letter, dated *Aug.* 25, 1766, readily undertakes to do. Besides the *Narraganset Indians*, he visits also the other four adjacent Tribes, in each of which he hopes there are many very capable of Instruction, and ready to embrace the Christian Faith, whose great Confidence in him he studies to improve to their spiritual and temporal Advantage. In a Postscript dated *October* 22, 1766, he writes, that he was sent for, and visited a Place between 30 and 40 Miles from *New London*, where he continued three Days, preached to a very large and attentive Audience, baptized several Children, and founded a Church, several openly declaring for the Church of *England*. He is to revisit them soon, and hopes to give an agreeable Account of his Proceedings.

The

The Rev. Mr. *Scovil,* the Society's Miſſionary at *Waterbury, Weſtbury, Northbury,* and *New Cambridge* in *Connecticut,* in his Letter dated *July* 8, 1766, writes, that the Number of Families belonging to the Church in *Waterbury* and *Weſtbury* is 102, in *Northbury* 46, in *New Cambridge* 32 ; of Communicants in this Miſſion 261 ; of Children baptized in the preceding Year 64, beſides 3 at *Roxbury,* one of the late Mr. *Davies's* Pariſhes, where he officiates occaſionally, as others have done in ſeveral Parts of that Miſſion, ſince the Death of that worthy, pious, prudent, zealous, and laborious Miſſionary. Mr. *Scovil* has four Churches, in which he performs ſtated Duty, full enough for two Clergymen, if any Method could be found for their Support, which he hopes in due Time will be effected, as he thinks it impoſſible for a Clergyman, who has a Variety of Churches under his Care, ſo effectually to promote the important Cauſe of Religion as a reſident Miniſter might do.

The Rev. Mr. *Andrews,* the Society's Miſſionary at *Wallingford, Cheſhire, Meridan,* and *North Haven* in *Connecticut,* in his Letter dated *July* 1, 1765, writes, that in the preceding Year he baptized 27 Infants and 2 Adults ; that his Communions are large conſidering the Number of his Pariſhioners ; and that he has a moſt pleaſing Proſpect of being uſeful in his preſent Miſſion. In his Letter dated *January* 7, 1766, he mentions his taking a Journey to *Great Barrington,*

rington, at the Distance of near 100 Miles, and preaching there to a considerable Congregation, and baptizing 4 Children. On his Return, he preached at *Westbury*, and once since to a crouded Audience, at the Opening of a decent Church there. In his Letter dated *June* 25, 1766, he writes, that besides officiating on *Sundays* in the several Parishes of his Mission, and preaching Week-day Lectures, upon every convenient Occasion, where most wanted in his Cure, and out of it, upon every proper Invitation, he baptized in the preceding Year 1 Adult and 35 Children in his Mission, besides those at *Great Barrington*.

New York.

The Society have received two Letters from Sir *William Johnson*, Bart. his Majesty's Superintendant for *Indian* Affairs in *North America*, dated *Oct.* 8, and *Nov.* 8, 1766. In the First of these he gives the strongest Assurances of contributing to the utmost of his Power to the Aid and Support of the laudable Purposes of the Society's Institution, particularly, with regard to the civilizing and converting the *Indians* in those Parts. On this Head he is of Opinion, that a Mission established at the Lower *Mohawks*, with proper help, would draw the *Oneidas* and others thither for Learning; and the Missionary would besides have it in his Power to assist the Members of the Church here; but constant Residence and an
exemplary

exemplary Life muſt be expected from him to infure Succeſs. This Miſſion might be eſtabliſhed at the Upper *Mohawks*. But what he thinks an Object of ſtill greater Importance is the Converſion of the *Senecas*, who exceed 1000 Men, and their Neighbours are much more numerous to the Weſtward, who would follow their Example. To this End he recommends, that a Miſſion, or School, be eſtabliſhed under ſome good Divine about *Oneida*, or *Anondaja*, to either of which the *Senecas*, &c. might conveniently come. This Divine ſhould be aſſiſted by a good Catechiſt, and as there are ſome *Mohawk* Lads qualified to act as Uſhers, their Preſence would encourage the Reſt to reſort thither. So that in a ſhort Time ſome would be qualified to take Orders and return with Abilities and natural Intereſt to promote the Faith among the Reſt. This Sir *William* gives as a rough Sketch, on which he promiſes to enlarge at ſome other Time; and with a View further to promote it, he propoſes, with his Majeſty's Permiſſion, to uſe his Intereſt with the *Indians* to obtain a Grant of Lands at a reaſonable Price for the Uſe of ſuch an Eſtabliſhment, which will in Time produce a Revenue ſufficient to defray the Expences of ſo pious an Undertaking. The Society have directed their Thanks to be returned to Sir *William Johnſon*, for his great Attention to the Intereſts of Religion, and readily and chearfully concur in the whole of his Scheme of appointing Miſſionaries and Catechiſts to the *Indians*, as ſoon as

H   proper

proper Persons can be procured, and determine
likewise to give suitable Encouragement to such
Mohawk Lads as shall be recommended to act in
the Capacity of Ushers under the Missionaries
and Catechists. In his other Letter, Sir *William
Johnson* writes, that he has a large Tract of
choice Land, on which he has already settled
about 120 Families, for the most Part industrious
Germans, who are as yet too poor to support a
Minister. Since which he has made Choice of a
good Situation, within a Mile of his own House,
on a publick Road, where he is forming a Town.
Ten Houses are already finished and inhabited,
and the Town being in the midst of his Settlements will increase very fast. He has also built
a very neat Stone Church, which, from its Vici-
nity to the greatest Part of the Settlement, will
serve the Town and Neighbourhood; and he
only wants a good Clergyman to render his Plan
compleat, there being several People here of the
Church of *England*, and the greatest part of the
Germans, together with the whole rising Generation, would become of that Persuasion, if a
Clergyman was fixed here. He therefore requests
the Society to appoint a Missionary with a small
Salary, to which Sir *William* will gladly contribute, and furnish him with a House and good
Glebe, so that he may live very comfortably.
Such an Appointment, he is persuaded, would
answer many of the Society's Intentions, parti-
cularly, with regard to the *Indians*, of whom
there are here, for at least six Months in the
Year

Year, from 500. to 1000, and some constantly reside at this Place, who could not fail of receiving great Improvement. He believes the Establishment of a Mission here would be of so great Use to the *Indians*, to the *German* Settlers, and to the *English* Protestants, that he would rather take upon himself the Salary than suffer so good a Work to drop. He desires his Proposal may be communicated to some worthy Clergyman, whose Situation may not be convenient at Home; but would willingly have a Man of an affable Disposition, of a middle Age, zealous in the Discharge of his Duty, and of an exemplary Life, as distant from Gloominess as Levity. If he has a moderate Family, the better, as he may have many Opportunities of fixing them happily; and as the Perquisites of the Cure will be annually increasing, Sir *William* has Reason to think many a Clergyman would find his Situation much mended by accepting it. The Society have resolved to appoint a Missionary for *Johnson Hall*, and will endeavour to provide such an one as may answer Sir *William*'s Description.

The Rev. Dr. *Auchmuty*, Rector of *Trinity* Church in the City of *New York*, in his Letter dated *May* 5, 1766, incloses the Petition of the Inhabitants of *Poghkeepsie* in *Dutches* County, where a Clergyman is much wanted, recommends them to the Favour of the Society, and thinks Mr. *Beardsley* might be usefully employed in this extensive County. The Petitioners set forth, that they have, after many Attempts, raised a sufficient Sum to purchase a handsome Glebe, and will secure a certain Sum annually for the support of a Minister of the Church of *England* to officiate in four different Precincts alternately. These Precincts take in a Tract of about 24 Miles in Length and 20 in Breadth, the Care of which Mr. *Beardsley* is willing to undertake, which they earnestly intreat he may, be permitted to do, and may have such further Aid and Assistance from the Society as they shall think proper.

The Society, being informed, in a Letter from Dr. *Auchmuty*, dated *Nov.* 12, that the People in *Dutches* County chearfully comply with the Terms required of them, and that there are already 80 Church Families in the County, and many more expected, have agreed to establish a New Mission at *Poghkeepsie*, and consented to Mr. *Beardsley*'s Removal thither.

Upon the Representation of Sir *William Johnson*, in his Letter of *Oct.* 8, and of Dr. *Auchmuty*, in his Letter dated *Oct.* 24, 1766, together with the Petition of the Protestant Inhabitants in Communion with the Church of *England* in the Town of *Schenectady*, about 17 Miles from *Albany*, the Society have engaged to appoint a Missionary at that Place, it appearing, that there is but one Clergyman in all the extensive County of *Albany*, and that the Church People of *Schenectady* have purchased a Glebe Lot, and by Subscription, chiefly amongst themselves, erected a neat Stone Church.

New

New Jersey.

The Rev. Mr. *Evans*, the Society's Missionary at *Glocester* and *Waterford*, in his Letter dated *Feb.* 25. 1766, informs them of his safe Arrival at his Mission, the kind Reception he met with, and the pleasing Prospects he has before him. One Church is finished, called *Cole*'s Church, and he expected in a few Months to have another fit to officiate in at *Glocester* Town. His two Congregations of *Cole*'s Church and *Glocester* have taken a House for him, with about 12 Acres of Ground, on a Lease of 5 Years.

The Rev. Mr. *Isaac Brown*, the Society's Missionary at *Newark* and *Second River*, in his Letters dated *Jan.* 6, *April* 7, and *Oct.* 6, 1766, writes, that one Mr. *Dow*, a sober, sensible Man, has taken Care of the School at *Second River* almost ever since Mr. *Avery* left it. From *Oct.* 6, 1765, to *Oct.* 6, 1766, he baptized 38 white Children and 6 black, and 2 black Adults.

The Rev. Mr. *Cutting*, late the Society's Missionary at *New Brunswick* and *Piscataqua*, since removed to *Hempstead* on *Long Island* in the Province of *New York*, in his Letter dated *Nov,* 26, 1765; *July* 26, 1766, writes, that the Church at *New Brunswick* appears to increase in Numbers, many of the Presbyterians, who have no Teacher, attending divine Service. At *Piscataqua* Numbers of all Denominations attend Church, and appear serious. He performed

ed divine Service twice at *Morris Town*, about 30 Miles from *Brunswick*, where there is a considerable Number of Church People, who are qualifying themselves to implore the Assistance of the Society. The first Time he baptized 12, and the next Time 7 Children at that Place. As often as he could be spared from the Duties of his own Churches, he attended at distant Parts, where his Services were thankfully received. In the 14 Months preceding the Date of his last Letter, he baptized at *Brunswick* 28 white Children and 3 Adults, 7 Negro Children and 2 Adults. His Communicants here were 34. At *Piscataqua* he baptized 9 white Children and 2 Adults, 2 Negro Children and 4 Adults. His Communicants here were 8.

Pensylvania.

A Letter from the Rev. Mr. *Reading*, the Society's Missionary at *Apoquinimink*, in his Letter dated *Sept.* 5, 1766, returns Thanks for the Board's readily consenting to the Petitions for his Removal to *Trenton*; but desiring, for Reasons of a private and personal, as well as a religious Nature, to remain in his present Mission, where he is resolved to exert himself in the Cause of Religion with the same Assiduity and Diligence, as, through God's Assistance, he has been enabled to do for 20 Years past with good Success. His Mission is in a respectable State, and he has the Happiness to see his Labours
succeed

succeed as much to his Satisfaction as can reasonably be expected. From *Nov.* 18, 1765, to the Date of this, he baptized 63 Infants and 1 Adult. His Communicants are 54.

The Rev. Mr. *Inglis,* late the Society's Missionary at *Dover,* &c. in his Letter dated *December* 19, 1765, acquaints the Society, that he had taken Leave of his Mission, which he did with great Regret, as the most perfect Harmony had subsisted between him and his Congregations, who express their great Concern at Mr. *Inglis's* Removal, who had with unwearied Diligence discharged every Duty of his Function, and conducted himself on all Occasions in a Manner truly laudable and exemplary. Upon their Promise to do every Thing in their Power to make their Mission agreeable, the Society appointed two Missionaries to succeed Mr. *Inglis* in this extensive and laborious Cure, *viz.* the Rev. Messrs. *Giles* and *Wilson,* who were both unfortunately drowned in their Return to *America.*

Mr. *Inglis,* in his Letters dated *April* 19, *May* 1, and *July* 10, 1766, takes Occasion, from the melancholy News of Messrs. *Giles* and *Wilson's* Death, earnestly to request a speedy Supply of the Missions of *Dover* and *Mispillion.* The same Request is renewed by the Church-Wardens and Vestries of the several Parishes in these Missions. The Society, willing to grant their Petition, have appointed the Rev. Mr. *Magaw,* Missionary at *Dover* and *Duck Creek,*

and

and to take Care of the other Parts of Mr. *Inglis's*
Miffion, till another Minifter can be provided.
Mr. *Inglis* lately made a Vifit to his old Miffion,
preached at all the Churches formerly under his
Care, and baptized 3 white Adults and 28 Children, 1 black Adult, and 1 Child. From the
Time he entered upon the Miffion in *July* 1759,
to his leaving it in *December* 1765, he baptized
750 white Children and 6 black, 21 white
Adults and 2 black. His Communicants, when
he came firft to the Miffion, were only 49;
when he left it they were increafed to 114;
which Number, he thinks, might be doubled
in a little Time, were two faithful Miffionaries
fixed there, as the Society propofe.

The Rev. Mr. *John Andrews*, on the Petition
of the Inhabitants of *Suffex County* on *Delaware*,
and the Recommendation of the Rev. Dr. *Smith*,
Mr. *Peters* of *Philadelphia*, and many other
worthy Clergymen, is appointed Miffionary at
Lewes in the faid County.

The Rev. Mr. *Barton*, the Society's Itinerant
Miffionary in *Lancafter*, in his Letter dated *Jan.*
23, 1766, writes, that his Catechumens attend
regularly; and feveral of the young People of
his Congregation, who fhew uncommon Seri-
oufnefs in Matters of Religion, came to the
Lord's Table at *Chriftmas*, while many were
preparing to follow their Example at *Eafter*.
In the *September* preceding, Mr. *Barton* paid a
Vifit to Sir *William Johnfon* in the *Mohawk*
Country, about 350 Miles from *Lancafter*, and
                                                    had

had an Opportunity of acquainting himfelf with a State of the *Mohawk Indians,* and enquiring into the beft Methods of carrying the Gofpel into the *Indian* Country. He finds the *Mohawks* very willing to receive Inftruction, and Sir *William Johnfon,* who is univerfally efteemed for his Goodnefs of Heart, very defirous to intereft himfelf in their Converfion. The Society have fignified to Sir *William Johnfon* and Mr. *Barton,* their general Approbation of every Scheme for the Inftruction of the *Indians,* and their Readinefs to improve every Opportunity of forwarding fo good a Work, and defired them to point out what particular Method may moft effectually be purfued to this End. The Society have been favoured with Sir *William's* Anfwer, the Subftance of which is laid before the Publick in the former Part of this Abftract: Mr. *Barton's* Anfwer is come to Hand, and will appear in the next Year's Account.

North Carolina.

The Society have received two Letters from his Excellency Governor *Tryon,* Dated *Jan.* 29 and *Oct.* 1, 1766, wherein they learn, that feveral of the Gentlemen recommended by them are arrived fafe, and have been fettled by the Governor. The Rev. *Barnet,* whom he has received into his Family, and whofe Conduct he finds fuitable to his Function, is fixed by him at *Brunfwick:* Mr. *Micklejohn,* of whom he has

I   great

great Expectations, he has sent into *Rowan County*; and believes he shall establish Mr. *Morton* in *Northampton County*, to the Satisfaction of the Parish.

By Letters from the Rev. Mr. *Earl*, the Society's Missionary at St. *Paul*'s Parish, *Chowan County*, dated *Mar.* 26 and *Oct.* 12, 1766, it appears, that from *April* 1765, to *Oct.* 12, 1766, he baptized 107 Children and 2 Adults, and had 30 Communicants; that he preached nine Times in *Berkley* Parish, which is destitute of a Minister, and once in *Society* Parish, and baptized 171 Children and 6 Adults.

The Rev. Mr. *Reed*, the Society's Missionary in *Craven County*, in his Letters dated *Jan.* 14, and *July* 20, 1766, writes, that the School House is inclosed, but knows not when it will be finished, as the whole Subscription is expended. The Vestry have agreed to give Mr. *Tomlinson*, the Society's School-master, 12 *l. per Annum* for attending the Church at *Newbern*, when Mr. *Reed* is officiating at the several Chapels. By his *Notitia Parochialis* it appears, that from *June* 21, 1765, to *June* 21, 1766, he baptized 202 white Children and 4 Adults, and 9 black Children, and 297 have received the Sacrament of the Lord's Supper.

The Rev. Mr. *Barnet*, the Society's Missionary at *Brunswick*, in his Letter dated *Feb.* 3, 1766, writes, that being settled at *Brunswick*, the Residence of the Governor, he officiates occasionally in other Places. His Parish is about

60 Miles by 30. He had vifited feveral Times thofe Parts appointed by the Veftry, and baptized from *November* 12 to *January*, 60 white Children, 1 Adult Negro and 1 Child, and three Times adminiftered the Sacrament to 25 Communicants. New-Light Baptifts are very numerous in the fouthern Parts of this Parifh. The moft illiterate among them are their Teachers, and even Negroes fpeak in their Meetings. They have lately offered Mr. *Barnet* the Ufe of their Meeting-Houfe, where he purpofes to officiate once in two Months. His Excellency Governor *Tryon* has been pleafed to fubfcribe about forty Guineas towards finifhing the Church at *Brunfwick*, which is a handfome Brick Building, upwards of 71 Feet in Length.

South Carolina.

The increafing Expence of the Society in fupporting a Number of new Miffions lately eftablifhed, and many more which they have engaged to fupply as foon as they can, has made it neceffary to withdraw their Salaries from the few remaining Miffionaries in *South Carolina*, who will be no Sufferers by this Reduction of their Salary, as there is a Provifion made by the Laws of that Province, to make up their Allowance equal to what it was before.

I 2　　　　　Georgia.

Georgia.

The Rev. Mr. *Zouberbuhler*, the Society's Miſſionary at *Savannah*, in his Letter dated *May* 1,
1766, writes, that the Commiſſioners for building a new Church at this Place have 800 *l.* Sterling at Intereſt, at 8 *per Cent.* which will in
Time enable them to carry their Truſt into Ex-
ecution.   In the mean while the old Church is
rendered very commodious, by a Grant from the
Aſſembly of 300 *l.* Sterling towards Repairs and
erecting a Gallery, and the Preſent of an Organ,
made by Col. *Barnard* of *Auguſta.*

The Rev. Mr. *Frink*, the Society's Miſſionary
at *Auguſta*, in his Letters dated *Jan.* 13 and
April 9, 1766, writes, that the Church is juſt
finiſhed ; but is too ſmall to contain one Third
of the Inhabitants.   The Parſonage-Houſe is
not yet put in Repair, nor the Out-Houſes built
as deſigned, but are to be compleated as ſoon
as poſſible.   His Pariſhioners attend Church
with more Conſtancy, and pay a greater Regard
to the Lord's Day, than at his firſt Arrival.   He
has made ſome Attempts to inſtil the Principles of Chriſtianity into the *Checkeſaw Indians,*
but all to no Purpoſe, while many of the white
People are as deſtitute of a Senſe of Religion as
the *Indians* themſelves.   Many ignorant Baptiſt
Exhorters, Men of infamous Character, ſtroll
about the Country, and invade the Prieſthood
ſo far as to adminiſter the Sacrament of the
Lord's

• Lord's Supper to their deluded Hearers, and are very often plunging their Converts in the River *Savannah*, which they are pleafed to call the River *Jordan*. Mr. *Frink* has vifited the white People, who are fettled as far as the *Indian* Boundaries, and baptized feveral Children. In *February* laft he took a Journey to the *Carolina* Side of the River *Savannah*, vifited feveral Places, where *Germans, French* and *Irish* have lately fettled, and from thence proceeded as high as Fort *Charlotte,* near eighty Miles above *Augufta.* From *January* 13 to *April* 9, he has chriftened 17 Whites and 2 Blacks. He has at length found a proper Perfon to keep School, whofe Salary from the Government at Home is 12 *l.* the reft is made up by Subfcription. *Edward Barnard,* Efq; of this Place, propofes to pay for the Inftruction and Cloathing of fix Children; which Example, it is hoped, will be followed by others. *Francis Macartan,* Efq; has made a Prefent of a genteel Cufhion for the Pulpit, with Hangings for that and the Reading-Defk.

The Society have this Year eftablifhed a Miffion at St. *John*'s, and appointed the Rev. Mr. *Alexander* Miffionary to that Place, on the Recommendation of his Excellency *James Wright,* Efq; Governor of the Province.

Bahama Iflands.

The Rev. Mr. *Carter,* whofe Affairs have called him to *London,* having fignified his Defire

fire to refign the Miffion of the *Bahamas*, after fifteen Years faithful Labours in thefe Iflands, the Society have appointed the Rev. Mr. *Tizard* Miffionary at *New Providence*, and the Rev. Mr. *Mofs*, Miffionary at *Harbour Ifland* and *Eleuthera*, where they are in great Want of religious Inftruction.

Africa.

The Rev. Mr. *Philip Quaque*, the Society's Miffionary, Catechift, and School-mafter to the Negroes on the Gold Coaft, in his Letter dated *Feb.* 23, 1766, acquaints the Society with his fafe Arrival at his Miffion. He thinks he has a Profpect of doing much Good here, by the Countenance and Affiftance of his Father *Caboßheer Cudjo,* who has promifed to get together as many young People for Inftruction as he can. The People are continually coming to him to know when he fhall open School, that they may bring their Children to be inftructed, and exprefs great Satisfaction that he is at laft come among them to fhew them the Way to eternal Life. *Caboßheer Cudjo* returns his fincere Thanks to the Society for the Care they have taken in the Education of his Son, and promifes to contribute all that lies in his Power to convince them that their Expence has not been in vain. And Mr. *Quaque* affures the Society, that he will, by the Grace of God take Care to difcharge his Truft with Fidelity, and hopes the Almighty

Almighty will influence his Heart, infpire him with true Zeal, and make him a happy Inftrument in converting many, who have hitherto wanted the Means of Inftruction.

☞ The Society, from their firft Inftitution, taking into their ferious Confideration the abfolute Neceffity there is, that thofe Clergymen, who fhall be fent Abroad, fhould be duly qualified for the Work to which they are appointed, defire every one, who recommends any Perfon to them for that Purpofe, to teftify their Knowledge, as to the following Particulars:

1. The Age of the Perfon.
2. His Condition of Life, whether fingle or married.
3. His Temper.
4. His Prudence.
5. His Learning.
6. His fober and pious Converfation.
7. His Zeal for the Chriftian Religion, and Diligence in his holy Calling.
8. His Affection to the prefent Government.
9. His Conformity to the Doctrine and Difcipline of the Church of *England.*

And the Society do now requeft, and earneftly befeech all Perfons concerned, that they recommend no Man out of Favour or Affection, or any other worldly Confideration, but with a fincere ſincere Regard to the Honour of Almighty GOD, and our bleſſed SAVIOUR; as they tender the Intereſt of the Chriſtian Religion, and the Good of Men's Souls.

And the Society particularly deſire their Friends in *America* to be ſo juſt to them, when any Perſon appears there in the Character of a Clergyman of the Church of *England*, but by his Behaviour diſgraces that Character, to examine as far as may be into his Letters of Orders, his Name and Circumſtances, and to inſpect the public Liſt of the Names of the Miſſionaries of this Society, publiſhed annually with the Abſtract of their Proceedings; and the Society are fully perſuaded it will appear, that ſuch unworthy Perſon came thither without their Knowledge; but if it ſhould happen, that any ſuch ſhould come thither from them, they intreat their Friends in *America*, in the ſacred Name of Chriſt, to inform them, and they will *put away from them that wicked Perſon.*

Barbadoes.

Barbadoes.

The Rev. Mr. *Butcher*, the Society's School-master at *Codrington-College*, in his Letter dated the 10th of *June*, 1766, writes, that the Number of the Boys on the Foundation is now compleat, being 18. Some of whom have made a confiderable Progrefs in Learning, and give good Hope, that they will fully anfwer the Society's Expectations. Some Books, according to Mr. *Butcher*'s Requeft, were fent laft Year for the Ufe of the School.

The Society's Attorneys, in their Letter dated *June* the 5th, 1766, write, that Mr. *Davies* having refigned his Station in the School, and Mr. *Thomas Duke* having declined to accept the Ufher's Place, they think themfelves very fortunate in having been applied to for that Office by the Rev. Mr. *Thomas Wharton*, a Gentleman of an unblemifhed Reputation, who for 12 Years hath had the chief Direction of a large and flourifhing Grammar-School in their Ifland with uninterrupted Succefs. On their Recommendation the Society have appointed Mr. *Wharton* to be the Ufher at *Codrington-College*.

K   The

The Receipts and Payments on the General Account of the Society for the Year paſt, ſtood thus at the Audit of the Society on the 29th Day of *January* 1767.

R E C E I P T S.

	l.	*s.*	*d.*
By Benefactions and Legacies and Entrance of Members in the Year 1766, — —	6019	13	0
By Subſcriptions of Members of the Society, — —	569	6	6
By Rent from Tenants, and by Dividends in the public Funds, — —	648	7	9
By Sale of Moneys in the public Funds, — —	1516	9	6
By Caſh of Mr. *Jennings* for the Purchaſe at *Annapolis*, formerly Governor *Nicholſon's*, ſold to *John Beale Bordley*, Eſq;	450	0	0
Total	9203	16	9

PAY-

PAYMENTS.

	l.	s.	d.
To the Treasurer the Ballance of his Account, *Jan.* 28, 1766,	2005	12	9
For Salaries to Missionaries, Catechists, Schoolmasters, and the Officers of the Society,	4173	14	8
For Books, Gratuities to Missionaries, and other incidental Charges,	268	4	5
To Monies laid out in the public Funds, and Legacies of this Year remaining there,	1396	4.	9
To Cash in the Hands of the Society's Treasurer, *Jan.* 29, 1767,	1360	0	2
Total	9203	16	9

K 2   Abstract

Abstract of the Society's *London* Account rela-
ting to *Codrington* College and their Plantations in *Barbadoes*, as ballanced by the Audi-
tors of the Society on the 29th Day of *Ja-*
nuary 1767.

The Society to the Trust Dr.

	l.	*s.*	*d.*
To Ballance of Accounts on the 28th Day of *January*, 1766,	956	13	6¼
To Nett Produce of 115 Casks of Sugar sold at *London*, ——	2147	1	4
To Dividends on 7000 *l.* Old South Sea Annuities for one Year due *October* 10, 1766,	210	0	0
To one Year's Dividend on 4000 *l.* Consol. Bank Annu- ities due *July* 5, 1766, ——	120	0	0
To 11 Months and 8 Days In- terest on 1600 *l.* *India* Bonds, to the 8th of *September*, 1766, Commission deducted, ——	52	4	11
To Sale of said *India* Bonds and Premium, —— —— —	1623	4	0
To Cash for 3000 *l.* Exchequer Bills paid off, and Interest thereon due, —— ——	3065	11	4
	£ 8174	15	1½

The

The Society to the Truſt Cr.

	l.	*s.*	*d.*
By Bills drawn at *Barbadoes* by the Society's Attorneys, and others, and paid here, ———	1227	17	5
By Salaries to Officers in *London*,	75	0	0
By Invoice of Goods ſent to *Barbadoes*, ——— ———	337	10	2
By Payment of Part of the Purchaſe of Mrs. *Whitaker*'s Eſtate at *Barbadoes*, ———	6231	1	10
By Caſh paid for the poor Sufferers by the Fire at *Boidge Town*, ——— ———	100	0	0
By Books ſent to *Codrington* College, and petty Diſburſements, —— —— ——	21	19	4
By Caſh in the Hands of the Society's Treaſurer, *Jan.* 29, 1767, ——— ———	180	19	4½
£	8174	15	1½

A LIST of the

MEMBERS

OF

The SOCIETY *for the Propagation of the Go*ſ*pel in Foreign Parts.*

Thoſe marked thus * were choſen Members in the Year 1766.

A.

THE Right Reverend *Richard* Lord Biſhop of St. *A*ſ*aph.*

Thomas Archer, M. A. Prebendary of *St. Paul's.*

Charles Ward Apthorp, of *New York,* Eſq;

John Apthorp, of *London,* Eſq;

James Apthorp, of *Bo*ſ*ton,* Eſq;

*Ea*ſ*t Apthorp,* M. A.

Mr. *Enos Alling,* of *New Haven, Conne*ᵭ*icut.*

The Rev. Dr. *Samuel Auchmuty,* Rector of *Trinity Church* in the City of *New York.*

The Rev. Sir *A*ſ*hur*ſ*t Allin,* Bart.

THE

B.

THE Right Reverend *Edward* Lord Bishop of *Bath* and *Wells*.

The Right Reverend *John* Lord Bishop of *Bangor*.

The Right Reverend *Thomas* Lord Bishop of *Bristol*.

The Honourable *Francis Barnard*, Efq; Governor of the Province of *Massachuset's Bay* in *New England*.

The Honourable and Reverend *Shute Barrington*, LL. D. Canon of *Christ Church*.

Richard Barford, D. D.

Edward Ballard, D. D.

Thomas Barnard, M. A. Rector of the Church of *Bridge Town* in *Barbadoes*.

The Rev. Mr. *James Barclay*.

Cutts Barton, D. D. Dean of *Bristol*.

John Bradstreet, Efq; Colonel.

Edward Bearcroft, Efq;

George Berkeley, M. A.

Edward Bernard, D. D. Provost of *Eton* College.

Jonathan Belcher, Efq; President of the Council in *Nova Scotia*.

John Berriman, M. A.

John Berney, D. D. Archdeacon of *Norwich*.

Calverley Bewicke, Efq;

Thomas Blackwell, M. A.

Ebenezer Blackwell, Efq;

Jonathan Blenman, Efq; Attorney-General in *Barbadoes*.

William

William Bowles, M. A. Fellow of *Winchester* College.

Robert Breton, M. A. Archdeacon of *Hereford*.

Henry Burrough, M. A. Prebendary of *Peter-borough*.

Joseph Browne, D. D. Provost of *Queen*'s College in *Oxford*.

John Burton, D. D. Fellow of *Eton College*.

Thomas Burton, D. D. Prebendary of *Durham*.

Philip Brown, B. D.

The Rev. Mr. *Bourdillon*.

Richard Bulkley, Esq; Secretary of the Province of *Nova Scotia*.

Joseph Banks, Esq;

* *John Benson*, M. A.

* *Walter Bagot*, M. A.

C.

THE most Reverend *Thomas* Lord Arch-bishop of *Canterbury*.

The most Reverend *Michael* Lord Archbishop of *Cashel*.

The Right Reverend *Charles* Lord Bishop of *Carlisle*.

The Right Reverend *Edmund* Lord Bishop of *Chester*.

The Right Reverend *William* Lord Bishop of *Chichester*.

The Right Honourable Lord *Colrayne*.

The Honourable *George Clinton*, Esq; Admiral.

L   *John*

John Chapman, D. D. Archdeacon of *Sudbury*.
Timothy Collins, M. A. Canon Refidentiary of
 Wells.
Mr. *John Cobb*.
Edward Codrington, Efq;
John Cookfey, M. A.
Charles Walter Congreve, M. A. Archdeacon of
 Armagh.
Allen Cowper, M. A.
John Craven, M. A.
Lewis Crufius, D. D. Prebendary of *Worcefter*.
Stephen Comyn, Efq;
William Henry Chauncey, Efq;
Colonel *Mordaunt Cracherode*.
Myles Cooper, M. A. Prefident of *King's College*
 at *New York*.
* *Richard Cuft*, D. D. Canon of *Chrift Church*,
 Oxford.

D.

THE moft Reverend *Charles* Lord Arch-
 bifhop of *Dublin*.
The Right Honourable *William* Earl of *Dart-*
mouth.
The Right Reverend and Honourable *Richard*
 Lord Bifhop of *Durham*.
The Right Reverend *Charles* Lord Bifhop of
 St. *David's*.
The Honourable *Wriothefley Digby*, Efq; LL. D.
Richard Dalton, Efq;

                                    Chriftopher

Chriſtopher Dawſon, Eſq;
Peter d'Eſpaignol, Eſq;
John Denne, D. D. Archdeacon of *Rocheſter.*
Samuel Dickens, D. D. Archdeacon of *Durham.*
George Dixon, D. D. Principal of *Edmund Hall*
 in *Oxford.*
Thomas D'oyly, LL. D. Archdeacon of *Lewis.*
Thomas Drake, D. D.
Robert Dinwiddie, Eſq;
* *David Durell,* D. D. Vice Chancellor of the
 Univerſity of *Oxford.*

E.

THE Right Reverend *Mathias* Lord Biſhop
 of *Ely.*
The Right Reverend and Honourable *Frederick*
 Lord Biſhop of *Exeter.*
Jucks Egerton, M. A.

F.

FREDERICK *Frankland,* Eſq;
 John Fountayne, D. D. Dean of *York.*
Tobias Frere, Eſq;
Thomas Edwards Freeman, Eſq;
Michael Franklin, Eſq; Lieutenant Governor of
 Nova Scotia.

G.

THE Right Reverend *William* Lord Biſhop
 of *Gloceſter.*
* The Right Hon. the Lord *Groſvenor.*

Henry

Henry Galley, D. D. Prebendary of *Glocester.*

William Geekee, D. D. Archdeacon of *Glocester.*

Edmund Gibson, M. A. Precentor of St. *Paul's.*

Benjamin Goodison, Esq;

John Gooch, D. D. Prebendary of *Ely.*

Sir *Francis Gosling*, Knt. Alderman of *London.*

David Gregory, D. D. Dean of *Christ Church*, *Oxon.*

Thomas Greene, D. D. Dean of *Salisbury.*

Blinman Gresley, M. A.

His Excellency *James Grant*, Esq; Governor of *East Florida.*

H

THE Right Honourable *George Montague Dunk*, Earl of *Halifax.*

The Right Honourable and Right Reverend Lord *James* Bishop of *Hereford.*

The Honourable and Reverend *John Harley*, M. A. Archdeacon of *Salop.*

The Honourable *James Hamilton*, Esq; Governor of *Pennsylvania.*

Hugh Hall, of *Boston* in *New England*, Esq;

James Hallifax, D. D.

George Harrison, of the City of *New York*, Esq;

Joseph Harrison, Esq; of *New Haven, Connecticut.*

Bartholomew Hammond, Esq;

Benjamin Hayes, Esq;

Mr. *George Hayter.*

John

John Head, D D. Archdeacon of *Canterbury.*

William Henry, D. D.

William Herring, D. D. Dean of St. *Afaph.*

Thomas Herring, M. A.

Samuel Holcombe, M. A. Prebendary of *Wor-cefter.*

Richard Hotchkis, M. A.

Jofeph Hudfon, Efq; Major General.

William Hutton, M. A.

William Hetherington, M A.

John Hotham, D. D. Archdeacon of *Mid-dlefex.*

The Honourable *Thomas Harley*, Efq; Alderman of *London.*

Thomas Hollingbery, M. A.

* *Richard Hind*, D. D.

I.

SIR *Edmund Ifham*, Bart.

Sir *Stephen Theodore Janffen*, Bart. Chamberlain of *London.*

Charles Jenner, D. D. Archdeacon of *Huntingdon.*

Laurence Jackfon, B. D. Prebendary of *Lincoln.*

Samuel Johnfon, D. D.

His Excellency *George Johnfon*, Efq; Governor of *Weft Florida.*

* Sir *William Johnfon*, Bart. his Majefty's Superintendant for *Indian* Affairs in *North America.*

THE

K.

THE Right Honourable *Thomas* Earl of *Kinnoul.*

Anthony Keck, Efq; Serjeant at Law.

Samuel Knight, M. A.

William Knox, Efq; Agent for *Georgia* and *Eaſt Florida.*

Benjamin Kennicott, D. D.

Joſhua Kyte, D. D.

L.

THE Right Reverend *Richard* Lord Biſhop of *London.*

The Right Reverend *Frederick* Lord Biſhop of *Litchfield* and *Coventry*, and Dean of St. *Paul*'s.

The Right Reverend *John* Lord Biſhop of *Landaff.*

The Right Reverend *John* Lord Biſhop of *Lincoln.*

The Right Reverend *William* Lord Biſhop of *Londonderry.*

The Reverend the Archdeacon of *London,* *John Jortin*, D. D.

The Right Honourable the Earl of *Lincoln.*

John Lawrey, M. A. Prebendary of *Rocheſter.*

William Lloyd, M. A.

Thomas Lloyd, D. D. Dean of *Bangor.*

John Lynch, D. D.

Edmund Lovell, M. A. Canon of *Wells.*

Thomas

Thomas Lane, Efq;
The Rev. Mr. *Chriftopher Lonfdale.*

M.

THE Right Honourable *Charles* Lord Vif-
count *Maynard.*

Margaret Profeffor of Divinity, *Oxon,* . *Thomas*
Jenner, D. D.

Margaret Profeffor of Divinity, *Cambridge,*
Zachary Brooke, D. D.

Alexander Macaulay, Efq;

William Markham, LL. D. Dean of *Rochefter.*

Offory Medlicot, M. A.

John Frederick Miege, D. D. Proteftant Ecclefi-
aftical Counfellor to the Elector *Palatine.*

Jeremiah Milles, D. D. Dean of *Exeter.*

John Meyonnet, D. D.

Gideon Murray, D. D. Prebendary of *Durham.*

Roger Moftyn, M. A.

Thomas Moore, D. D.

John Moore, M. A.

Charles Morton, M. D. and F. R. S.

John Morgan, B. D. Chancellor of St. *David's.*

Thomas Morifon, M. A.

Charles Martyn, M. A. of *South Carolina.*

The Honourable *James Murray,* Efq; Governor of all *Canada.*

N.

THE moft Noble *Thomas Holles* Duke of
Newcaftle.

The

The Right Reverend *Philip* Lord Biſhop of
    Norwich.
Gerard Neden, D D. Prebendary of *Lincoln*.
John Nicols, D. D. Preacher of the *Charter-*
    Houſe.
———— *Naſh*, M. A.
* Sir *Roger Newdigate*, Bart.

O.

THE Right Reverend *Robert* Lord Biſhop
    of *Oxford*.
The Honourable *James Oglethorpe*, Eſq; Lieute-
    nant General.
* *Newton Ogle*, D. D.

P.

THE Right Reverend *Robert* Lord Biſhop
    of *Peterborough*.
The Right Honourable Sir *Thomas Parker*, Lord
    Chief Baron of the *Exchequer*.
Vincent Perronet, M. A.
The Reverend *James Perard*, M. A. Chaplain to
    the King of *Pruſſia*.
Charles Plumptre, D. D. Archdeacon of *Ely*.
Edward Poole, M. A. Prebendary of *Brecknock*.
John Potter, D. D. Dean of *Canterbury*.
John Pownall, Eſq; Secretary to the Lords of
    Trade and Plantations.
The Hon. *Thomas Pownall*, Eſq; Governor of
    South Carolina.

Joſ.

Jof. Parfons, M. A.
Charles Pointz, M. A.
The Reverend Mr. *Richard Peters*, Rector of
 Philadelphia.
Colonel *Frederick Philips*, of *Philipfburg* in the
 Province of *New York*.
William Parker, D. D.
Edmund Proudfoot, Efq;

Q.

*N*UTCOMBE *Quicke*, LL. B. Chancellor
 of the Church of *Exeter*.

R.

THE Right Reverend *Zachary* Lord Bifhop
 of *Rochefter*, and Dean of *Weftminfter*.
The Right Honourable the Earl of *Radnor*.
Sir *Thomas Robinfon*, Bart.
Thomas Randolph, D.D. Prefident of *Corpus Chrifti*
 College, and Archdeacon of *Oxford*.
Regius Profeffor of Divinity, *Oxford*, *Edward
 Bentham*, D. D.
Regius Profeffor of Divinity, *Cambridge*, *Thomas
 Rutherforth*, D. D.
John Richards, LL. D.
William Richardfon, D. D. Mafter of *Emmanuel*
 College, *Cambridge*.
William Robinfon, Efq;
Mr. *John Rofs* of *Philadelphia*.

M

John

John Rutherford, M. A.
John Rotheram, M. A.
William Rivet, Efq;

S.

THE Right Reverend *John* Lord Bifhop of *Salifbury.*

The Honourable *William Shirley,* Efq; Governor of the *Bahama Iflands.*

Samuel Salter, D. D. Mafter of the *Charterhoufe.*

Erafmus Sanders, D. D. Prebendary of *Rochefter.*

George Secker, D. D. Canon Refidentiary of St. *Paul's*

Jonathan Shipley, LL. D. Dean of *Winchefter.*

William Smith, D. D. Provoft of the College of *Philadelphia.*

Samuel Stedman, D. D. Prebendary of *Canterbury.*

Adlard Squire Stukeley, Efq;

Joseph Sims, M. A. Prebendary of St. *Paul's.*

John Simpfon, M. A.

Alexander Steadman, Efq; Chief Juftice of the Common Pleas in *Philadelphia.*

Sir *William Stephenfon,* Knt. Alderman of *London.*

* ——— Shinton, D. D.

T.

SIR *John Thorold,* Bart.
   Thomas Tanner, D. D. Prebendary of *Canterbury.*

Mr. St. *George Talbot,* of *New York.*
John Tatterfall, M. A.
Edmund Tew, D. D.
John Thomlinfon, Efq;
John Thomlinfon, jun. Efq;
James Torkington, M. A.
Hugh Thomas, D. D. Dean of *Ely.*
John Thomas, LL. D. Prebendary of *Weftminfter.*
John Thornton, Efq;
Sir *John Torriano,* Knt.
Chauncey Townfhend, Efq;
Thomas Tounfon, B. D.
Barlow Trecothick, Efq; Alderman of *London.*
Jofiah Tucker, D. D. Dean of *Glocefter.*
Charles Tarrant, D. D. Dean of *Peterborough.*
John Temple, Efq; Surveyor General of the Cuf-
    toms in the North Diftrict of *America.*
Samuel Turner, Efq; Alderman of *London.*
John Townfon, Efq;
* His Excellency *William Tyron,* Efq; Governor
    of *North-Carolina.*
* *Edward Tew,* M. A.

V.

*P*HILIP *de Valois,* M. A.
    Henry Vane, D. D. Prebendary of *Durham.*
Abbot Upfher, M. A.

The

The Rev. Mr. *Vaughan*, Chaplain to the Factory at *Hamburgh*.

W.

T HE Right Reverend *John* Lord Bishop of
        Winchester.
The Right Reverend *James* Lord Bishop of
    Worcester.
The Right Reverend *Richard* Lord Bishop of
    Waterford.
The Honourable *Benning Wentworth*, Esq; Go-
    vernor of *New Hampshire* in *New England*.
Francis Walwyn, D. D. Prebendary of *Canter-
    bury*.
Henry Waterland, LL. D. Prebendary of *Bristol*.
John Waugh, D. D. Dean of *Worcester*.
John Wilberfofs, Esq;
Christopher Wilson, D. D. Canon Residentiary of
    St. *Paul's*.
Thomas Williams, of *Merthyr*, Prebendary of
    Brecknock.
Edward Wilson, M. A.
Thomas Wilson, D. D. Prebendary of *Westminster*.
Granville Wheeler, M. A.
Thomas Crome Wickes, D. D.
John Waring, M. A.
George Woollaston, M. A.
George Walker, Esq; Agent for *Barbadoes*.
William Worthington, D. D.

THE

Y.

THE moſt Reverend *Robert* Lord Archbiſhop
of *York*, Lord Almoner.

Francis Yarborough, D. D. Principal of *Brazen-
Noſe* College, *Oxford*.

Edward Yardley, B. D. Archdeacon of *Cardigan*.

LADIES

LADIES Annual Subſcribers.

LADY *Curzon.*
  The Honourable Mrs. *Shirley.*
Mrs. *Cotton* of *Etwall* in *Derbyſhire.*
Miſs *Cordelia Bright.*
Mrs. *Gordon.*
Mrs. *Sydenham.*
The Honourable Mrs. *George Talbot.*
Mrs. *Elizabeth Torriano* of *Kenſington.*
Mrs. *Margaret Floyer,* of *Dorcheſter.*
Mrs. *Ann Maynard.*
Mrs. *Vic* of *Clifton.*
Miſs *Palmer.*

A LIST

A LIST of the

BISHOPS, DEANS, &c.

Who have PREACHED before

The SOCIETY *for the Propagation of the Gospel in Foreign Parts.*

Anno.

1701 THE Reverend Dr. *Willis*, Dean of Lincoln.

1702 The Lord Bishop of *Worcester*, Dr. *Lloyd*, not printed.

1703 The Lord Bishop of *Sarum*, Dr. *Burnet*.

1704 The Lord Bishop of *Lichfield* and *Coventry*, Dr. *Hough*.

1705 The Lord Bishop of *Chichester*, Dr. *Williams*.

1706 The Lord Bishop of St *Asaph*, Dr. *Beveridge*.

1707 The Reverend Dr. *Stanley*, Dean of St. *Asaph*.

1708 The Lord Bishop of *Chester*, Sir *William Dawes*.

1709 The Lord Bishop of *Norwich*, Dr. *Trimnel*.

1710 The Lord Bishop of St. *Asaph*, Dr. *Fleetwood*.

1711 The Reverend Dr. *Kennet*, Dean of *Peterborough*.

1712 The Lord Bishop of *Ely*, Dr. *Moore*.

1713 The Reverend Dr. *Stanhope*, Dean of *Canterbury*.

1714 The Lord Bishop of *Clogher*, Dr. *Ash*.

1715 The Reverend Dr. *Sherlock*, Dean of *Chichester*.

1716 The Reverend Mr. *Hayley*, Canon Residentiary of *Chichester*.

1717 The Lord Bishop of *Hereford*, Dr. *Biffe*.

1718 The Lord Bishop of *Lichfield* and *Coventry*, Dr. *Chandler*.

1719 The Lord Bishop of *Carlisle*, Dr. *Bradford*.

1720 The Reverend Dr. *Waddington*.

1721 The Lord Bishop of *Bristol*, Dr. *Bolter*.

1722 The Reverend Dr. *Waugh*, Dean of *Glocefter*.

1723 The Lord Bishop of *Ely*, Dr. *Greene*.

1724 The Lord Bishop of St. *Afaph*, Dr. *Wynn*.

1725 The Lord Bishop of *Glocefter*, Dr. *Wilcocks*.

1726 The Lord Bishop of *Norwich*, Dr. *Leng*.

1727 The Lord Bishop of *Lincoln*, Dr. *Reynolds*.

1728 The Lord Bishop of *Hereford*, Dr. *Egerton*.

1729 The Reverend Dr. *Pearce*.

1730 The Reverend Dr. *Denne*, Archdeacon of *Rochester*.

1731

1731 The Reverend Dr. *Berkeley*, Dean of *Londonderry*.

1732 The Lord Bishop of *Lichfield* and *Coventry*, Dr. *Smallbrooke*.

1733 The Reverend Dr. *Maddox*, Dean of *Wells*.

1734 The Lord Bishop of *Chichester*, Dr. *Hare*.

1735 The Reverend Dr. *Lynch*, Dean of *Canterbury*.

1736 The Lord Bishop of St. *David's*, Dr. *Clagget*.

1737 The Lord Bishop of *Bangor*, Dr. *Herring*.

1738 The Lord Bishop of *Bristol*, Dr. *Butler*.

1739 The Lord Bishop of *Glocester*, Dr. *Benson*.

1740 The Lord Bishop of *Oxford*, Dr. *Secker*.

1741 The Reverend Dr. *Stebbing*, Chancellor of *Sarum*.

1742 The Lord Bishop of *Chichester*, Dr. *Mawson*.

1743 The Lord Bishop of *Landaff*, Dr. *Gilbert*.

1744 The Reverend Dr. *Bearcroft*, Secretary of the Society.

1745 The Lord Bishop of *Bangor*, Dr. *Hutton*.

1746 The Lord Bishop of *Lincoln*, Dr. *Thomas*.

1747 The Lord Bishop of St. *Asaph*, Dr. *Lisle*.

1748 The Reverend Dr. *George*, Dean of *Lincoln*.

1749 The Lord Bishop of St. *David's*, Dr. *Trevor*.

1750 The Lord Bishop of *Peterborough*, Dr. *Thomas*.

1752 The Lord Bishop of *Carlisle*, Dr. *Osbaldiston*.

N   1753.

1753 The Lord Bishop of *Landaff*, Dr. *Cresset*.

1754 The Lord Bishop of St. *Asaph*, Dr. *Drummond*.

1755 The Lord Bishop of *Norwich*, Dr. *Hayter*.

1756 The Lord Bishop of *Lichfield* and *Coventry*, Dr. *Cornwallis*.

1757 The Lord Bishop of *Chester*, Dr. *Keene*.

1758 The Lord Bishop of *Glocester*, Dr. *Johnson*.

1759 The Lord Bishop of St. *David's*, Dr. *Ellis*.

1760 The Lord Bishop of *Chichester*, Dr. *Ashburnham*.

1761 The Lord Bishop of *Landaff*, Dr. *Newcome*.

1762 The Lord Bishop of *Oxford*, Dr. *Hume*.

1763 The Lord Bishop of *Bangor*, Dr. *Egerton*.

1764 The Lord Bishop of *Peterborough*, Dr. *Terrick*.

1765 The Lord Bishop of *Norwich*, Dr. *Yonge*.

1766 The Lord Bishop of *Glocester*, Dr. *Warburton*.

1767 The Lord Bishop of *Landaff*, Dr. *Ewer*.

The Form of a LEGACY to this SOCIETY.

ITEM, *I give to* the Incorporated SOCIETY, for the Propagation of the Gofpel in Foreign Parts, *the Sum of*   *to be raifed and paid by and out of all my ready Money, Plate, Goods, and Perfonal Effects, which by Law I may or can charge with the Payment of the fame* (and not out of any Part of my Lands, Tenements, or Hereditaments) *and to be applied towards carrying on the Charitable Purpofes for which the faid Society was Incorporated.*

N. B. The Variation in this Form of a LEGACY, from that formerly printed, is made neceffary, on Account of fome unhappy Miftakes in Wills, by which feveral confiderable Legacies have been loft to the Society, and the good Intentions of the Teftators have been intirely defeated, becaufe the Sums bequeathed to the Society have been ordered to be raifed, or paid out of Lands, or Real Eftates, which is not now permitted by Law.

Direct to *Edward Pearfon*, Efq; in *Duke Street, Weftminfter*, their TREASURER.

And to the Reverend Dr. *Daniel Burton* in *Abingdon Street, Weftminfter,* their SECRETARY.

On the imperfect Reception of the Gospel.

A

SERMON

Preached before the

Incorporated SOCIETY

FOR THE

Propagation of the Gospel in Foreign Parts;

AT THEIR

ANNIVERSARY MEETING

IN THE

Parish Church of St. Mary-le-Bow,

On FRIDAY *February* 17, 1769.

By *THOMAS NEWTON*, D. D.
Lord Bishop of *BRISTOL.*

LONDON:
Printed by E. OWEN and T. HARRISON in
Warwick-Lane.
MDCCLXIX.

At the Anniverſary Meeting. of the Society for *the* Propagation of the Goſpel in Foreign Parts, *in the* Veſtry-Room *of St.* Mary-le-Bow, *on* Friday *the* 17th *Day of* February, 1769.

AGREED, that the Thanks of the SOCIETY be given to the Right Reverend the Lord Biſhop of *Briſtol*, for his Sermon preached this Day before the SOCIETY; and that his Lordſhip be deſired to deliver a Copy of the ſame to the SOCIETY to be Printed.

Daniel Burton, Secretary.

JOHN X. 16..

Other sheep I have which are not of this fold.

THERE is a scruple which one time or other ariseth in the breast, I believe, of every serious considerate Christian; and That is, How cometh it to pass that the Christian religion is professed only in so small a part of the world, while Paganism and Mohammedism overspread at least three quarters of the globe? Since *there is none other name under heaven* Acts. iv. *whereby men must be saved,* why is any other 12. name under heaven adored, besides the name of Christ Jesus? Why doth God suffer imposture

to prevail so far over truth, the kingdom of
Satan over the kingdom of his dear Son?
Jer.xii.1. *Righteous art thou, O Lord, when we plead with*
thee, yet let us talk with thee of thy judgments.

1. Suppoſing we cannot give any ſatisfactory
account of this proceeding, yet it is not therefore a juſt objection againſt the providence of
God. It muſt be confeſſed, that the imperfect
reception of Chriſtianity in the world is one of
the darkeſt myſteries of divine providence; but
becauſe we cannot readily apprehend the rea-
ſons of God's government, ſhall we therefore
conclude it to be conducted without reaſon?
How can our finite groveling minds fully un-
derſtand the polity of the ſupreme infinite
Pſ.xxxvi. mind? *His judgments are like the great deep,*
6. not to be fathomed by the ſhort line of human
reaſon. How do we know what mercy God
may extend to thoſe who have not heard of the
high-prieſt of our profeſſion Chriſt Jeſus?
How do we know but he ſuffers not the goſpel
to be preached to ſeveral nations, as knowing
before hand that they would reject it, and by
theſe means aggravate their condemnation?
Expedients there may be to ſolve this difficulty
more than man can expreſs, more than he can
Rom. xi. imagin. *O the depth of the riches both of the wiſ-*
33, 34. *dom*

dom and knowlege of God! How unfearchable are his judgments, and his ways paft finding out! For who hath known the mind of the Lord, or who hath been his counfeller? However of this we may reft affured, that God can as foon ceafe to be, as ceafe to do what is beft and fitteft in the whole: and though *clouds and darknefs are* Pf. xcvii. *round about him, yet righteoufnefs and judgment* ²· *are the habitation of his feat ;* though we cannot enter into the reafons of his difpenfations, nor comprehend all the various methods of his dealing with the fons of men, yet infinite juftice muft act juftly, infinite wifdom muft act wifely, and infinite goodnefs muft do things which are good and right to be done.

2. But God was not obliged to make a revelation of himfelf univerfal. That God made any revelation of himfelf at all was an act of mere bounty, mercy, and goodnefs; and furely he may confer his favors in what manner, and at what times, and upon what perfons he pleafeth. *I will be gracious* (faith the Lord) Exod. *to whom I will be gracious, and will fhow mercy* xxxiii. 19. *on whom I will fhow mercy.* God was no more obliged to make all men Chriftians, than he was to make all creatures men, or all men angels : and as he hath manifefted his power and

wifdom

wifdom in induing different perfons with different tempers and capacities, why might he
not as well afford to fome more and greater,
to fome fewer and lefs opportunities of know-
Mat. xx. ing and ferving him? *Is, it not lawful for him*
15. *to do what he will with his own? Hath not the*
potter (as the Apoftle argueth on this head)
Rom. ix. *power over the clay, of the fame lump to make*
21. *one veffel to honor, and another unto difhonor?*

3. As God was not obliged to make a revelation of himfelf univerfal, fo he hath foretold
by the mouth of his holy prophets, that the
Chriftian religion fhould not (for fome time
at leaft fhould not) be univerfal. And what
more pregnant, more convincing proofs can
we require of this, than thofe many prophecies of the obftinacy and infidelity of the
Jews in the Old Teftament, of the diftreffes
and perfecutions of the Chriftians in the New?
So that the want of univerfality is fo far from
infringing the truth of the Chriftian religion,
that it is abfolutely neceffary, we fee, to confirm it; as that without which thefe prophecies, and confequently the books containing thefe prophecies, could not be true.

4. But though God make not a revelation
univerfal, yet hath he not left himfelf *without*
witnefs.

witness. Though the scriptures be not put into every man's hands, yet the larger volumes of nature and right reason lie ever open to all mankind. There is such grandeur and exquisite contrivance, such beauty and proportion in this great fabrick of the universe, as evidently point out to us the first cause, the all-wise and all-powerful architect. Every thing within us, every thing without us, may lead us one way or other to the knowlege of God and of our duty: and if men however are blindly hurried away by their lusts and passions, and listen not to the dictates of nature and the whispers of conscience, they are *without excuse,* and their condemnation will be, that having eyes they would not see, and having understandings they would not understand. Herein I speak the sense of the great preacher to the Gentiles, who declares, that, *though God suffered all nations to walk in* Acts xiv. *their own ways, nevertheless he left not himself* 16, 17. *without witness, in that he did good, and gave us rain from heaven and fruitful seasons, filling our hearts with food and gladness:* And in another place speaking of the Gentiles he saith, *That* Rom. i. *which may be known of God is manifest in them,* 19, 20. *for God hath showed it unto them; For the invisible things of him from the creation of the world*

                                                                        are

are clearly seen, being understood by the things that are made, even his eternal power and godhead, so that they are without excuse.

5. Though a revelation be made to some persons only, yet it may be of great service to many others. Christianity operates beyond the sphere of Christendom. At the first rising of the sun of righteousness many even of the Heathens were sensibly reformed, and became better and brighter as it were by reflection. They grew ashamed of their former barbarous rites and superstitious ceremonies; and no longer made use of human sacrifices, no longer offered their sons and their daughters unto devils. It is also very well worth our observation, that morality hath been carried to a greater highth, and the law of nature hath been more rationally explained, illustrated, and inforced by many a one of the philosophers since the coming of Christ, than by all of them taken together before it. And if there is any thing good and excellent in the false religions of the world, it is wholly borrowed from some traditions of the true religion, or derived from that fountain of goodness and excellency, the holy scriptures. Of such signal advantage is the Christian institution even to Pagans and unbelievers; and

like

like its divine author, *blesseth* its very *enemies*, and doeth *good to them* who *despitefully use* it and *persecute* it.

6. Christ's satisfaction upon the cross was not partial but universal. He died for all mankind in general, as well for those who went before, as those who come after him; as well for those who have not, as those who have, opportunities of knowing him. He is for this reason stiled in scripture *the Saviour of the world.* He is upon this account said to *give himself a ransom for all,* and to *taste death for every man.* He is by St. John called *the propitiation for our sins, and not for our sins only, but also for the sins of the whole world.* As all 1 Tim. ii. 6. Hebr. ii. 9. 1 John. ii. 2. men were created by him, so by him were all redeemed: as all men were involved in the consequences of Adam's transgression, so all partake of the benefits of Christ's righteousness; or to speak in the words of St. Paul, *as by the offence of one judgment came upon all men to condemnation, even so by the righteousness of one the free gift came upon all men unto justification of life.* Rom. v. 18.

7. Men will be judged variously, in proportion to their various means and opportunities of knowing and doing their duty. For

B   what

what juftice would it be to expect the fame returns of duty and obedience from the rude Indian in his hutt, or wild favage in the woods, as from thofe who have had the advantage of a learned and Chriftian education, who *from children have known the holy fcriptures,* and *have been taught as the truth is in Jefus?* Far be it from God, to require impoffibilities of any man, or to condemn any man for invincible ignorance. The words of Rom. ii. St. Paul are very clear in this point, *As many* 12. *as have finned without law, fhall alfo perifh without law; and as many as have finned in the law,* Rom. iv. *fhall be judged by the law:* and afterward, *Where* 15. *no law is, there is no tranfgreffion;* where a law is not fufficiently promulged, there men are not accountable for the violation of it. Our Luke xii. Saviour and Judge himfelf faith, *Unto whom-* 48. *foever much is given, of him fhall be much required; and to whom men have committed much,* John. ix. *of him they will afk the more:* and again, *If ye* 41. *were blind, ye fhould have no fin; but now ye fay We fee, therefore your fin remaineth.*

8. There is fcarce any civilized nation, that hath not one time or other had fufficient opportunity of being converted to the Chriftian religion. Our Saviour's inftruction to his

difciples

disciples was, *Go teach all nations :* and the _{Mat.}
writers of the history of the church all with ^{xxviii.19.}
one full consent and entire harmony agree,
that the apostles or their immediate disciples
in their own persons published the glad ti-
dings of the gospel through all the parts of
the world then known. St. Paul himself very
aptly applies to them the elegant saying of the
Psalmist, *Their sound went into all the earth,* Rom. x.
and their words into the end of the world. 18.
Within about five centuries after Christ we
find the fathers asserting, that * the Christians
were in all parts of the world far more numerous than both the Heathens and Jews.
Nay even in these degenerate times we shall
have no reason to think, that the unbelievers
are left wholly destitute of the means of coming to the knowlege of the truth ; considering that the Christians are of all people the
most learned, and hold trade and commerce
with all ; considering again that there are
some Christians or others dwelling in every

* *Plures enim jam Christiani sunt, quam si Judæi simula-*
crorum cultoribus adjungantur. St. Aug. de Utilitate credendi.
Cap. 19. Tom. 8. Edit. Benedict. &c. &c.

country,

country, and in all Mohammedan countries
the Chriftian religion is in the higheft degree
of efteem next to their own ; confidering farther that there are focieties erected for the
propagation of the gofpel, and miffionaries dif-
patched into feveral remote parts of the world ;
confidering laftly that there are extant, in all
the current languages of the world, tranflations
of the Bible, which are fo many pipes and
conduits as it were to convey knowlege
unto all people.

9. That the gofpel therefore is not more
generally profeffed muft be charged altogether upon the faults of men, and not in the
leaft imputed to want of forefight or goodnefs
in God. In the propofing of a new revelation
God dealeth with us like (what he hath made
us) free reafonable creatures. He commits
no violence upon our faculties, but addreffeth
himfelf coolly to our underftandings. He af-
fords fuch evidences of the truth as are fufficient indeed, but not fuch as are irrefiftible ;
fuch as may eafily convince us if we will, but
not fuch as muft and fhall convince us whether we will or not. Such is the reafonable-
nefs evidence and certainty of the Chriftian
religion, that I am verily perfuaded whoever

ever calmly confiders the arguments urged in defenfe of it cannot but fee and acknowlege its divine origin, believe without doubt and affent without referve. Whence is it therefore that it doth not find a more general reception? Whence is it that fo many withftand its force? Why? becaufe they are too idle or too bufy to confider; they think not of it at all, or think with prejudice; they have bad heads or corrupt hearts. Why in particular did the Jews reject the Chriftian religion? Becaufe they were eaten up with blind zeal and bigottry for their law; and the expectations of a temporal prince had fo poffeffed and fwelled their minds, that they could not relifh the humble doctrins of the crofs. Why ftill did not the Greeks embrace it? Becaufe they were proud opionative men, and fought after (what they falfely called) *wifdom*; and as Chrift crucified was to the *Jews a ftumbling block*, fo was he to the *Greeks foolifhnefs*. Why are fo many nations which once were Chriftian become Anti-chriftian? Becaufe they did not *bring forth the fruits of the gofpel,* and therefore *the candleftick of the Lord was removed out of its place, and the kingdom of God was taken from them.* Why has Mohammedifm prevailed fo
mightily

1 Cor. i. 22, 23.

See Mat. xxi. 23. Rev. ii. 5.

mightily in the world? It is plain the grounds
upon which that impofture ftandeth are the
vices and follies of men; it was begot by am-
bition and luft, was propagated by rapin and
violence, and is ftill upheld by power and au-
John iii. thority.   And thus though *light is come into*
19.   *the world, men love darknefs rather than light,*
becaufe their deeds are evil.   I wifh I could not
add that Chriftianity hath been ftopt and re-
tarded in its progrefs by the herefies and
fchifms of fome, the debauched lives and con-
verfations of others, who profefs themfelves
Chriftians, but yet are really a fcandal to the
doctrin of Chrift.   Had Chriftian princes been
as ambitious of extending the kingdom of
Chrift, as of enlarging their own empires;
had Chriftian fubjects been as zealous to propagate the gofpel as to carry on traffick and
commerce; and had the lives of all been agreeable to their moft holy profeffion, the Chriftian
religion would not have been confined within
1 Pet. ii. thefe narrow bounds, and thofe who now *fpeak*
12.   *againft us as evil doers,* would then, *beholding*
our good works, have glorified God in the day of
vifitation.

    10. This very want of univerfality is made
to ferve feveral wife ends and purpofes of providence.

vidence. Such is the tranſcendent wiſdom of God, that he can bring good out of evil, light out of darkneſs, and turn even the infidelity of ſome into arguments to beget and nouriſh faith in others. None of the philoſophers and princes of the world embraced Chriſtianity till ſome centuries after Chriſt : *not many wiſe, not* 1 Cor. i. *many mighty, not many noble were called*; for what reaſon? *that no fleſh ſhould glory in his pre-ſence*, that the propagation and eſtabliſhment of the goſpel might appear not to be owing to hu-man means, but to be the work of heaven itſelf. The infidelity of the Jews renders them per-haps more proper and unſuſpected witneſſes of the truth of the Old Teſtament, than if they had been converted to Chriſtianity; for the conceſſions of a profeſſed enemy generally carry greater force and conviction with them, than the moſt favorable arguments urged by a friend. The more too are the enemies of our religion, the more is the divine providence manifeſted in preſerving his church, and not ſuffering *the* Mat. xvi. *gates of hell to prevail againſt it.* Had *this* 18. *counſel or this work been of men,* it would doubt- Acts v. leſs, in ſo many ages, amidſt ſo many enemies, 38, 39. have *come to nought,* but *being of God, nothing can overthrow it.*

Laſtly,

Laftly, It is foretold in fcripture, that the Chriftian religion fhall one time or other before the end of the world become univerfal. This, I think, is plainly intimated in the words following my text; *Other fheep I have,* faith our bleffed Saviour, *which are not of this fold; them alfo I muft bring, and they fhall hear my voice, and there fhall be one fold and one fhepherd.* Hitherto, I conceive, are to be referred

Pf. ii. 8.
Pf. lxxii. 11.
Dan. vii. 14.

thofe promifes of giving Chrift *the heathen for his inheritance, and the uttermoft parts of the earth for his poffeffion;* of *all kings falling down before him;* and of *all people, nations, and languages ferving him.* *When the fulnefs of the*

Rom. xi. 25, 26.

Gentiles is come in, faith St. Paul, *all Ifrael fhall be faved.* Many and triumphant are the predictions of this kind; for there is no fubject upon which the prophets dwell more, or more delight to dwell. At what time and by what methods God will accomplifh this wondrous revolution, we cannot fay; but accomplifh it he will, as furely as he is true. *Hath he faid,*

Numbers xxiii. 19.

and fhall he not do it? Hath he fpoken, and fhall he not make it good?

No doubt there are more and greater reafons than thefe known to that all-perfect mind which governs the univerfe: but even thefe

(upon

(upon each of which I might have expatiated, but have compreſſed the matter into as narrow compaſs as I could) if not ſingly taken, yet all united, are I hope of force ſufficient to lay the objection, and to ſatisfy us that God may be juſtified in his tranſactions, even in the moſt dark and myſterious of his tranſactions, with the ſons of men : *as it is written, that thou* Rom. iii. *mighteſt be juſtified in thy ſayings, and mighteſt* 4. *overcome when thou art judged.*

The natural conſequence of this diſcourſe is the great duty of promoting, as much as lieth in our power, the univerſal reign of Chriſt upon earth. For the imperfect ſtate of Chriſtianity is no juſt objection to divine providence ; it is more properly a reproach to ourſelves, and condemns the negligence and indifference of Chriſtians. We are aſſured indeed by God himſelf ſpeaking in the prophet, *From the riſing* Mal.i.11. *of the ſun even unto the going down of the ſame my name ſhall be great among the Gentiles, and in every place incenſe ſhall be offered unto my name, and a pure offering ; for my name ſhall be great among the Heathen, ſaith the Lord of hoſts:* But we muſt not ſit idle and unconcerned ſpectators waiting for the accompliſhment of this prediction, under pretence of leaving it to the

C ſuperior

superior wifdom and almighty power of God. He intends all his predictions to be accomplifhed by the agency of men; and happy are thofe men, who fhall be the agents and inftruments of effecting what providence fo gra-cioufly intends, and who fharing in the heavenly work fhall be fure alfo to fhare in the heavenly reward.

We are taught to pray daily, and I fuppofe every one almoft doth pray daily, *Thy kingdom come*; but it is not enough to offer up our prayers, unlefs we likewife exert our moft zealous endevors; for how can we be thought to pray in earneft, as long as we do nothing more ? Not that I conceive we are obliged with the hazard of our lives and fortunes to propagate the gofpel in foreign parts; neither muft we feek the advancement of our religion by pious leagues and holy wars, by ftriving to regain with our fwords thofe countries which we have loft by our fins. We are by no means fit for the one, and the other is not fit for us. We are not indued with the gift of tongues and the power of miracles neceffary for the 2 Cor. x. former; and as for the latter *the weapons of our* 4. *warfare are not carnal but fpiritual.* The fpirit indeed of Croifades prevailed mightily for fome centuries, and fet all the princes of Chriftendom

in

in arms. But we have not fo learned Chrift; and would we contribute fomething to the extenfion of the Chriftian name we muft endure conflicts, and obtain victories of another kind. To fight under the banner of Chrift againft fin the world and the devil; to conquer and fubdue our rebellious lufts and appetites; to *caft down imaginations, and every high thing that* exalteth itself againft the knowlege of God; to bring our paffions into fubjection to our reafon; to have the free and uncontrolled empire of our minds; to let *the peace of God rule in our hearts;* thefe are the wars, thefe are the triumphs of Chriftians. The beft way to enlarge the kingdom of Chrift without us, is firft to begin by planting and eftablifhing it within us. For how can we expect that others fhould be won over to our belief, when we ourfelves live as if we believed not? *Let your light fo fhine before men that they may fee your good works, and* the confequence will be, *they will glorify your Father which is in heaven.*

2 Cor. x. 5.

Col. iii. 15.

Mat. v. 16.

The Chriftian religion is fo falutary and beneficial a fcheme, fo plainly calculated for the fervice and intereft of mankind as well as for the honor and glory of God, that it is an act of the greateft humanity and charity to plant and culti-

C 2

vate

vate it, wherever we have any opportunity :
and to fee how happy kingdoms and nations
are with it, and how miferable they are for
the want of it, we need only compare the
former florifhing ftate of the churches of Afia
and Africa with their prefent wretched condition, now they are funk in fuperftition and
ignorance, in flavery and brutality. What
barbarians were the people of this iland, before ever the light of the gofpel fhone upon
them; and how have we been improved and
civilized fince in confequence of it ? And do
we not find in our colonies and plantations
abroad, that the people grow lefs and lefs favage, and more and more humanized, in proportion as true Chriftianity is propagated and
prevails more among them ?

    However it may be in other places, here
Mat. ix. certainly *the harveft is plenteous, but the laborers*
37, 38. *are few; pray ye therefore the Lord of the har-*
veft, that he will fend forth laborers into his har-
veft. We are the more obliged to this tender
care and concern for them, as we receive fo
many benefits and advantages from thence;
and as we *reap* of their *carnal things*, it is but
2 Cor. ix. juft and equitable that we fhould *fow* unto
11. them of our *fpiritual things.* How many have
                                   large

large properties there, and go thither to carry on traffic and commerce; and shall none be found to propagate true religion and virtue among them? The worst of our species, felons and convicts, are transported thither in abundance; and shall we send none of a better character to give them better ideas of us and our religion? The church of Rome glories in the zeal and number of her missionaries, who *compass sea and land to make proselytes;* and shall they be more diligent to propagate a false Christianity than we the true? And if we totally neglect our colonies and plantations, will they not soon sink into barbarism and brutality, or become an easy prey to fanaticism, or popery, or infidelity, or atheism, or what not?

But *how then shall they believe in him, of whom they have not heard? and how shall they hear without a preacher? and how shall they preach except they be sent?* Rom. x. 14. 15. Small contributions can hardly be applied at all, and larger benefactions will avail little and lose their effect applied separately; nothing considerable can be done, no great information be gained, no great influence be preserved, but under the direction and conduct of a regular society.

Such

Such a fociety was accordingly erected and incorporated near feventy years ago by a Prince,
to whom our religion and liberties owe their prefervation : and its primary and immediate object
was (according to the words of the charter) *the*
maintenance of a learned and orthodox clergy for
the adminiftration of the word and facraments
in thofe of our colonies and plantations, where
was either mean provifion or none at all for
the public worfhip of God. The defign was
truly pious and charitable, and God hath
bleffed it with remarkable fuccefs. For in
thofe countries, where they had fcarcely any
form or place of public worfhip; where even
the Lord's day was hardly diftinguifhed from
others but by greater idlenefs and profanenefs;
where the facraments were adminiftered, bap-
tifm perhaps not above once in twenty years, and
the Lord's fupper not above once in fixty : there
more than a hundred churches have been erected, and more are erecting; there more than
a hundred and forty thoufand of our people,
infants and adults, have been baptized; there
more than a hundred and fifty thoufand bibles and common-prayer-books, with other
pious and inftructive treatifes and fmaller tracts
innumerable, have been diftributed; many

                                              nume-

numerous congregations have been set up, who maintain the public service of God at their own expense; and the Society are at the farther charge of more than a hundred missionaries catechists and schoolmasters for the farther propagation of the gospel and instruction of the young and ignorant. So that now there is a goodly appearance of religion; much good hath been done, and possibly more harm prevented; the people are greatly reformed and improved; and it is * computed that one third of the inhabitants, near a million of souls, are professed members of the church of England.

Another and an early object of the Society's attention were the poor Negroes, whose bodily labor and service justly intitle them to some concern for their spiritual welfare. It was not long after the first institution of the Society, that instructions were given to the missionaries for this purpose, and catechists and schoolmasters were employed, and have proceeded in this good work of teaching and baptizing these Heathen slaves, as far as the difficulty of the thing, and their Christian or rather unchristian masters would allow. From

* See Dr. Bradbury Chandler's Appeal to the Public in behalf of the Church of England in America, Sect. 6.

that

that time to this many, thousands of them
have been converted to the faith; and they
have upon all occasions behaved better, with
more fidelity and duty, than their unconverted
brethren; whenever any insurrections and re-
bellions have happened, few or none of the
Christian Blacks have been concerned in them.
It would be little for the honor of the Society
to exhort and admonish others, if they did not
themselves, within their own property and
plantations, set a good example to other planters and masters, in the management of their
Negroes, softening the severities of their ser-
vitude, treating their persons with gentlenefs,
as well as forming their minds by seasonable
instruction, rightly conceiving humanity to
be one of the most effectual methods of con-
ciliating them to Christianity: and it is much
to be wished, that the example was more generally followed. A farther improvement
hath been made by the Society within these
few years, by giving some kind of liberal education to some young Negroes, and training
them up in such a manner as may qualify
them to become more familiar teachers and
instructors of their countrymen; an expedi-
ent, which it is hoped, will be attended
with

with confiderable fuccefs both in Africa and America.

After thefe more immediate objects of their care and attention, fome fhare of the Society's compaffion hath been extended to the native Indians : and notwithftanding the diverfity and difficulty of their languages, their wandering life, their grofs ignorance, their fierce difpofitions, their continual wars, their favage manners, their barbarous cuftoms, their horrid fuperftitions, yet feveral of them have been made converts, and fome congregations of Chriftians have been formed among the Mohawks and other Indian tribes. Some of the Society's miffionaries and catechifts have been at the pains of learning fome of the American languages for the readier difcourfe and communication with the people; and fome fchools are erecting for their better education and inftruction, to civilize in order to convert them.

But yet the defigns of the Society are very far from being completed. Many things are wanting to perfect and eftablifh the good work that is begun. With regard to the members of the church of England, they are continually importuning the Society to fend over more miffionaries, more than their abilities will

D allow,

allow, which is a certain indication that many advantages have arisen from those who have been sent already. But the greatest want of all is that of an American Bishop for the purposes of confirmation, ordination, visitation of the clergy, and other ecclesiastical offices, without the least share of civil power or jurisdiction whatever. Such an institution patronized by so many pious and judicious persons living and dying, and especially by the late most worthy ever to be lamented ever to be honored President of this Society, but indeed what good design did he not patronize and encourage? Such an institution, I say, may be beneficial to many, can be really hurtful to none: and shall all other sectaries enjoy their particular privileges and forms of worship in their full latitude, and at the same time the members of the national church, near a million of souls as I said, a third of the people, be debarred and deprived of what they esteem so material a part of their constitution? Where is the justice, equity, or reason of this proceeding? But there are men who will receive neither law nor gospel from us; who clamor for liberty, but yet are the most imperious of task-masters and tyrants; who contend

tend

tend for the moſt unlimited toleration for themſelves, but yet are to all others moſt intolerant, wherever they get power into their own hands.

With regard to the poor Negroes, whoſe number is * computed to be conſiderably above half a million; as it is now generally known and underſtood that Chriſtianity maketh no alteration in mens civil rights and conditions, but *every man* is to *abide in the ſame calling* 1 Cor. vii. *wherein he was called,* whether he be bond or 20. free; it is to be hoped that the proprietors and planters will be leſs jealous of their ſlaves being inſtructed in the true religion, which will ſoften and improve their manners, and make them ſubject not only for fear but alſo for conſcience ſake, *with good will doing ſervice, as to* Eph. vi. *the Lord, and not to men.* Whatever neceſſity 7. may be pleaded for it, it is greatly to be lamented, that there is any ſuch thing as ſlavery any where. As Moſes ſaid, *Would God that* Num. xi. *all the Lord's people were prophets,* ſo I would 29. ſay, Would God that all mankind were free, that thoſe who are bond were free, and that thoſe who are free may ſo uſe their liberty as not to abuſe it unto licentiouſneſs!

* See Dr. Chandler as before.

D 2   With

With regard to the native Indians; a wide
field is opened to us by the late treaty of peace.
But they muſt be made men, before they can
be made Chriſtians.   To bring them off from
their roving courſes, and reconcile them to a
more ſettled kind of life; to give them ſome
notions of agriculture, and furniſh them with
proper implements for it; to teach them ſuch
of the more common mechanic arts, as may
be the means of their more comfortable ſub-
ſiſtence; to open ſchools in different parts for
their farther erudition and improvement; to
learn their languages, or familiarize them to
our own; to convince them of our concern
for their ſpiritual by our regard to their temporal welfare, by acts of humanity juſtice and
kindneſs; theſe will be found to be the moſt
efficacious methods of winning them over to
our religion, of *turning them from darkneſs to*
light, and from the power of Satan unto God,
that they may receive forgiveneſs of ſins, and
inheritance among them which are ſanctified.

Acts xxvi. 18.

Great things have already been done by the
Society, though their certain annual income is
a trifle compared to their certain annual ex-
penſe; but greater ſtill remain to be done,
which indeed can never be accompliſhed without

out the charitable contributions of well-dif-
poſed perſons, without the aid and aſſiſtance of
government, and without the particular bleſſing
of Almighty God. May God Almighty therefore ſo diſpoſe the hearts, and open the hands
of you and of all to whom this charity ſhall
be recommended, that it may go on proſper-
ing and to proſper; that *the word of the Lord* 2 Theſ.
may have free courſe, and be glorified; that *his* iii. 1.
way may be known upon earth, his ſaving health Pſ. lxvii.
among all nations; that *the kingdoms of this* Rev. xi.
world may become the kingdoms of our Lord and 15.
*of his Chriſt ; and he may reign for ever and
ever !*

An

An ABSTRACT of the

CHARTER,

And of the Proceedings of the SOCIETY for the Propagation of the Gospel in Foreign Parts, from the 19th Day of *February*, 1768, to the 17th Day of *February*, 1769.

KING *William* III. of Glorious Memory, was graciously pleased, on the 16th of *June*, 1701, *to erect and settle a Corporation with a perpetual succession, by the name of* THE SOCIETY FOR THE PROPAGATION OF THE GOSPEL IN FOREIGN PARTS; *for the receiving, managing, and disposing of the contributions of such persons as would be induced to extend their charity towards* the Maintenance of a Learned and an Orthodox Clergy, *and the making of such other provision as might be necessary for the Propagation of the Gospel in Foreign Parts, upon information, that in many of our Plantations, Colonies, and Factories beyond the seas, the provision for Ministers was mean, and many other of our said Plantations, Colonies, and Factories, were wholly unprovided of a maintenance for Ministers, and the publick Worship of God; and that, for lack of support and maintenance*

of

of *such, many of his loving subjects wanted the administration of God's word and sacraments, and seemed to be abandoned to Atheism and Infidelity, and others of them to Popish superstition and idolatry.*

The Society was composed, by the Charter, of the Chief Prelates and Dignitaries of the Church, and of several other Lords, and eminent persons in the State, with a power to elect such others to be Members of the Corporation, as they, or the major part of them, should think beneficial to their charitable designs; and they immediately applied themselves with great zeal and alacrity to the good work; and after adjusting preliminaries in the choice of Officers, and settling standing orders and rules for their more regular proceeding, they subscribed every one of them according to their several ranks and dispositions, an annual sum to be paid to their Treasurer, for the general uses of the Society; and chose new Members, and gave out deputations according to the powers in the Charter, to receive and collect the donations of all charitable and well-disposed persons towards this most pious design: And thro' an especial blessing, *this work of the Lord hath* hitherto *prospered in their hands.* Many more than one hundred and forty thousand of our own people, infants and adults, and many thousands of *Indians* and *Negroes,* have been instructed and baptized into the true faith of our Lord Jesus Christ; and more than one hundred

hundred and fifty thousand volumes of bibles and common prayer books, with other books of devotion and instruction, together with an innumerable quantity of pious small tracts, have been dispersed in foreign parts; and there is now a very hopeful and improving appearance of religion in the public worship of God, according to the liturgy of the Church of *England*, in a great number of churches in our plantations in *America*, by the means, and through the procurement, of this Corporation.

The charter directs the Society to give an annual account to the Lord High Chancellor, the Lord Chief Justice of the *King's Bench*, and the Lord Chief Justice of the *Common Pleas*, of the several sums of money by them received, and laid out, and of the management and disposition of the revenues of the corporation: This is punctually done, and the Society annually make public an Abstract of them and their proceedings. Therefore the Society now, in the first place, acknowledge the receipt, and return their most hearty thanks for the particular benefactions of the year 1768, *viz.*

	l.	*s.*	*d.*
To Mrs. *Leigh*, of *Northcote*,	1	1	0
The Hon. *Thomas Fitzmaurice*, Esq;	1	1	0
To Sir *Thomas Worsley*, Bart.	1	1	0
To *David Urry*, Esq; ———	1	1	0
To the Rev. Dr. *Walker*, Rector of Motestone, —— —— }	1	1	0

E   To

	£	s	d
To the Rev. Mr. *Oglander*, —	1	1	0
To the Rev. Mr. *Troughear Holmes*	1	1	0
To *Robert Pope Blachford*, Efq;	1	1	0
To the Rev. Mr. *Culme*, Rector of *Freshwater*, —	1	1	0
To the Rev. Mr. *Walton*, Rector of *Brixton*, —	1	1	0
To *Robert Worsley*, Efq; —	0	10	6
To *William White*, Efq	0	10	6
To Mr. *Clark*, of *Newport*, —	0	10	6
To Mr. *Leigh*, of *Thorleigh*,	0	10	6
To the Rev. Dr. *Knail*, Vicar of *Carisbrook*, by whom the above-mentioned Benefactions were remitted,	1	1	0
To a Lady, defiring to be unknown, by Dr. *Tew*, —	1	1	0
To the Hon. Mrs. *George Talbot*, by Mr. *Thomas Lewis*, —	5	5	0
To the Right Hon. Lady *Jane Edwards*, of *Tickencote*, in *Rutland*, by the Rev. Mr. *Wilson*, Vicar of *Empingham*,	1	1	0
To a Lady, defiring to be unknown, by the Lord Archbifhop of *Canterbury*,	5	8	0
To Lady *Curzon*, —	5	5	0
To *Gerard Arme Edwards*, Efq; by the Rev. Mr. *Wilson*, —	1	1	0
To a Lady unknown, by the Rev. Mr. *Broughton*, —	20	0	0
To a Perfon unknown, by Mr. *Stonefreet*, —	2	2	0
To a Member who defires to be unknown, —	3	3	0

For

For the Legacy of Mrs. *Elwes*, late of *Chifwick*, in *Middlefex*, from *Cary Elwes*, Efq; by the Hands of Mr. *Walter Dicker*.	1200	0	0
To a Lady unknown, by the Rev. Dr. *John Burton*, ———	I	I.	0
To *Charles Jennens*, Efq; of *Gopfal*, in *Leicefterfhire*, by the Hands of Mr. *Hetherington*, ——— ———	21	0	0
To Mrs. *Elizabeth Hanmer*, by Mr. *Hetherington*, ———	5	5	0
To Mrs. *Fowler*, ——— —	10	10	0
To a Clergyman in the Eaft of *Suffex*, by the Rev. Mr. *Wilfon*, —	I	I	0
To Mrs. *Catharine Kelfey*, ———	2	2	0
To Mrs. *Frances Pearce* ———	2	2	0
To Mrs. *Tyrrell*, of *Ormond-Street*, by the Hands of the Rev. Dr. *Plumptree* —— ——	10	0	0
To a Lady unknown, ———	5	5	0
To Lady *Anne Shadwell*, ———	2	2	0
To Dr. *William Powel*, of *Nanteos*, *Pembrokefhire*, —— ——	I	I	0
To *Anthony Eglington*, Efq;	50	0	0
To the Rev. the Dean of *York*, and feveral other Perfons, —	23	17	6
To the Rev. Mr. *Thompfon*, of *Elham*,	I	I	0
To Mrs. *Sufannah Mathew*, —	I	I	0
To a Lady unknown, by *Thomas Pearce*,	10	0	0
For the Legacy of Mrs. *Elizabeth Woodroffe* of *Bury St. Edmund's*, *Suffolk*, Widow, by her Executors,	400	0	0

To

To Mrs. *Barkhurst*,	100	0	0
To Mrs. *Catharine Palmer*, her annual Subscription,	2	2	0
To *Roger Pratt*, Esq; of *Riston*, in *Norfolk*, by the Rev. Dr. *Dering*,	5	5	0
To a Lady unknown by Mr. *Venn*,	50	0	0
To Miss *Sydenham*,	4	4	0
To *Henry Southby*, Esq; of *Caversham*, *Oxfordshire*,	1	1	0
To the Rev. Sir *Ashurst Allin*, Bart. being a Collection in his Parishes,	2	2	0
To *Robert Luson*, Esq; of *Blundeston*, by Sir *Ashurst Allin*, Bart.	0	10	6
To a Person unknown, by *A. P.*	10	0	0
For the Legacy of *Jonathan Taylor*, Esq; by his Executors,	137	2	11
For the Legacy of *John Williams*, by *John Vincent*, Executor,	20	0	0
For the Legacy of Mrs. *Mary Stacey*, by Mr. *Totton*,	50	0	0
To the Rev. Mr. *Lambert*,	50	0	0
For the Legacy of *Stephen Skinner*, Esq; of *Colchester*, by his Executor, Mr. *William Hazledine*, of *Watford*,	100	0	0
To a Gentleman of *Louth*, in *Lincolnshire*, by his Friend in *London*,	2	2	0
To a Lady unknown, by the Rev. Mr. *Pritchard*, Reader at *South-Audley* Chapel,	5	5	0
For the Legacy of *Robert Fraser*, by his Executors,	10	10	0

To

To a Lady unknown, by *William Robinfon*, Efq;	2	2	0
To the Rev. Mr. *Fenwicke*, of *Hallaton*, near *Harborough*, *Leiceſterſhire*,	1	1	0
To Mrs. *Bewicke*, by Mr. *Fenwicke*,	3	0	0
To Mrs. *Sarah Carte*, by Mr. *Fenwicke*,	1	1	0
For the Legacy of Dr. *Stephen Niblett*, by his Executor, *John White*, D. D.	50	0	0
To *E. I. W.*	9	0	0
To a Perſon unknown, by the Rev. Dr. *Head*,	2	2	0
To the Hon. Mrs. *Shirley*,	5	5	0
For the Legacy of *Dorothy Randolph*, by her Executor, *John Tetlow*,	10	0	0
To a Lady unknown, by the Rev. Mr. *Hotchkiſs*,	2	2	0
To Mrs. *Dollyffe*, by Dr. *Cruſius*,	2	2	0
For the Legacy of *Samuel Anderſon*, by his Executors, *James Jacks* and *Joſeph Thornthwaite*,	50	0	0
To the late Mrs. *Vicx*, by Dr. *Tucker*, Dean of *Glouceſter*,	5	5	0
To a Lady unknown, by Dr. *Tucker*,	5	5	0
To the Rev. Mr. *Marrian Feaver*, of *Dorſetſhire*,	1	1	0
To a Lady unknown, by Dr. *Tew*,	1	1	0
To a Perſon unknown, by the Rev. Mr. *Taylor*,	5	5	0
To Mrs. *Elizabeth Torriano*, of *Kenſington*,	5	5	0
To Mrs. *Lucy Oſborne*	2	2	0

Theſe

Thefe benefactions, together with fix pounds, fix fhillings, paid at entrance of new members, amounting to the fum of two thoufand five hundred, and twenty-four pounds, fixteen fhillings, and eleven pence, are all the benefactions to the Society, brought to account for the year 1768; all which, and a much larger fum, amounting in the whole to the fum of four thoufand two hundred and feventy-two pounds, two fhillings and eight pence halfpenny, has been expended in falaries, gratuities to miffionaries, and other incidental charges, and for books fent by the Society to *North America,* where the Society have erected feveral new miffions, and employed more fchool-mafters.

N. B. Befides thefe, the following benefactions which came too late for the audit of the Society's accounts in *January* 1768, and being paid during the vacancy of the Treafurer's office were omitted in the laft audit, are carried to account in the Society's fund, and will be added to the balance in the Treafurer's hands next year, *viz.*

To an unknown Lady, by Mr. *Tilbury,* — —	30	0	0
To Mr. *Lane,* — —	100	0	0
To Mrs. *Dollyffe,* by Dr. *Crufius,*	2	2	0
To the Rev. Mr. *Taylor,* of *Clifton,*	5	5	0

The

The Names of the Society's Miffionaries, Catechifts and School-mafters, with their refpec-
tive falaries, are as follow:

Newfoundland.

Annual Salaries.
£.

1 Mr. *Langman*, Miffionary at St. *John's Town*, } 50

2 Mr. *Balfour*, Miffionary at *Trinity Bay*, 50

3 Mr. *Coughlan*, Miffionary at *Harbour Grace* and *Carboneer*, } 50

4 Mr. ⸻ School-mafter at *Harbour Grace*, } 10

Nova Scotia.

5 Mr. *Breynton*, Miffionary at *Halifax*, 70
6 Mr. *Lynch*, School-mafter at *Halifax*, 10
7 Mr. *Wood*, Miffionary at *Annapolis Royal*, and *Granville*, } 70
8 Mr. ⸻ School-mafter at *Annapolis*, 10
9 Mr. *Morifon*, School-mafter at *Granville*, 10
10 Mr. *Moreau*, Miffionary to the *French* at *Lunenburgh*, } 70
11 Mr. *Bailly*, School-mafter to the *French* at *Lunenburgh*, } 15
12 Mr. *Bryzelius*, Miffionary to the *Englifh* and *Germans* at *Lunenburgh*, } 70
13 Mr. *Neuman*, School-mafter at *Lunenburgh*, } 10

14 Mr.

14 Mr. *Bennet*, Missionary at *Horton*, *Windsor*, *Newport*, *Falmouth*, and *Cornwallis*, } 70

15 Mr.   School-master for *Horton* and *Cornwallis*, ——— ——— } 10

16 Mr. *Watts*, School-master for *Windsor* and *Newport*, ——— ——— } 10

17 Mr. *Eagleson*, Missionary in the County of *Cumberland*, ——— } 70

New England.

Province of New Hampshire.

18 Mr. *Arthur Browne*, Missionary at *Ports-mouth*, - ——— ——— ——— } 60

————————— for officiating at *Kittery*,   15

19 Mr. *Badger*, Itinerant Missionary in *New Hampshire*, ——— ——— } 50

Province of Massachuset's Bay.

20 Mr. *Bailey*, Itinerant Missionary on the Eastern Frontiers, ——— ——— } 50

21 Mr. *Wheeler*, Missionary at *George Town*, and places adjacent, on *Kennebeck* river, ——— ——— } 40

22 Mr. *Wiswall*, Missionary at *Falmouth* in *Casco Bay*, ——— ——— ——— } 20

23 Mr. *Bass*, Missionary at *Newbury Port*,   50

24 Mr. *Weeks*, Missionary at *Marblehead*   50

25 Mr. *Macgilchrist*, Missionary at *Salem*,   50

26 Mr. *Serjeant*, Missionary at *Cambridge*,   50

27 Mr.

27 Mr. *Winflow*, Miffionary at *Braintree*, 60
28 Mr. *Ebenezer Thompfon*, Miffionary at Scituate and *Marfhfield*, —— } 50
29 Mr. *Clarke*, Miffionary at *Stoughton*, and *Dedham*, —— —— } 20

Colony of Rhode Ifland.

30 Mr. *Marmaduke Browne*, Miffionary at *Newport*, — —— — } 50
31 Mr. *Fayerweather*, Miffionary at *Nara-ganfet*, —— — } 50
32 Mr. *Ufher*, Miffionary at *Briftol*, 60
33 Mr. *John Graves*, Miffionary at *Provi-dence*, —— —— } 50
—————— for officiating at *Warwick*, 15
34 Mr. *Taylor*, School-mafter at *Providence*, 10

Colony of Connecticut.

35 Dr. *Johnfon*, Miffionary at *Stratford* and *Milford*, —— — — } 50
36 Mr. *Newton*, Miffionary at *Ripton*, 30
37 Mr. *Lamfon*, Miffionary at *Fairfield*, 50
38 Mr. *Dibblee*, Miffionary at *Stamford*, 50
39 Mr. *Mathew Graves*, Miffionary at *New London*, — — — — } 60
40 Mr.   School-mafter to the *Nara-ganfet Indians*, —— —— } 15
41 Mr. *John Beach*, Miffionary at *Newtown* and *Reading*, —— — — } 50
42 Mr. *Hubbard*, Miffionary at *New Haven* and *Weft Haven*, —— } 40

F   43 Mr.

43 Mr. *Gibbs*, Miſſionary at *Simſbury* and Hartland,   — — — } 30

44 Mr. *Viets*, Aſſiſtant to Mr. *Gibbs*,   20

45 Mr. *Mansfield*, Miſſionary at *Derby* and Oxford, — — — } 40

46 Mr. *Leaming*, Miſſionary at *Norwalk*,   50

47 Mr. *Clarke*, Miſſionary at *New Milford*, *Woodbury*, *Kent*, *New Fairfield*, and *Sharon*, — — — } 30

48 Mr. *Palmer*, Miſſionary at *Litchfield*, *Cornwall*, and *Great Barrington*, } 30

49 Mr. *Scovil*, Miſſionary at *Waterbury*, *Weſtbury*, *Northbury*, and *New Cambridge*, — — — } 30

50 Mr. *Peters*, Miſſionary at *Hebron*,   30

51 Mr. *Andrews*, Miſſionary at *Wallingford* *Cheſhire*, *Meridan*, and *North Haven*, } 20

52 Mr. *Tyler*, Miſſionary at *Norwich*,   30

New York.

53 Mr. *Cutting*, Miſſionary at *Hempſtead* on Long *Iſland*, — — } 30

54 Mr. *Avery*, Miſſionary at *Rye*, —   40

55 Mr.   School-maſter at *Rye*, —   10

56 Mr. *Charlton*, Miſſionary at *Staten Iſland*, 50

57 Mr. *Egberts*, School-maſter at *Staten Iſland*, — } 15

58 Mr. *Samuel Seabury*, Miſſionary at *Eaſt* and *Weſt Cheſter*, — — } 40

59 Mr. *George Youngs*, School-maſter at *Weſt Cheſter*, — — } 10

60 Mr.

60 Mr.   Missionary at *Schenectady*,   30

61 Mr. *Munro*, Missionary at *Albany*, and
   to the *Mohawk Indians*,   ——   } 50

62 Mr. *Oël*, Assistant in instructing the
   Indians,   ——   —— } 10

63 *Paulus*, a *Mohawk*, School-master to
   the *Indians*,   ——   —— } 7 10

64 Mr. *Sayer*, Missionary at *Newburgh*,   30

65 Mr. *Hildreth*, School-master at *New*
   York,   ——   ——   —— } 15

66 Mr. *Beardsley*, Missionary at *Pogh-*
   keepsie, in *Dutches* County,   —— } 35

67 Mr. *Townsend*, Missionary at *Salem*, in
   West Chester County, and Places adjacent,   ——   —— } 40

New Jersey.

68 Dr. *Chandler*, Missionary at *Elizabeth*
   Town,   ——   —— } 50

69 Mr.   Missionary at *Amboy*
   Woodbridge,   ——   —— } 50

70 Mr. *Odell*, Missionary at *Burlington*,
   and *Mountholly*,   —— } 50

71 Mr. *Lyon*, Missionary at *Glocester* and
   Waterford,   ——   —— } 40

72 Mr. *Cooke*, Missionary in *Monmouth*
   County,   ——   —— } 60

73 Mr. *Isaac Browne*, Missionary at
   Newark,   ——   —— } 50

74 Mr. *Abraham Beach*, Missionary at
   New Brunswick and *Piscataqua*, } 40

75 Mr.

75 Mr. *Stewart,* School-master at *Second River,* — — 10

76 Mr. *Ayres,* Missionary at St. *Peter's Spotswood,* and St. *Peter's Freehold,* 40

77 Mr. *William Thomson,* Missionary at *Trenton* and *Maidenhead,* — 50

78 Mr. *Frazer,* Missionary at *Amwell, Kingwood* and *Musconetcunck* — 40

Pennsylvania.

79 Mr. *Ross,* Missionary at *Newcastle,* — 60

70 Mr. *Reading,* Missionary at *Apoquinimink,* 60

81 Mr. *Craig,* Missionary at *Chester,* — 60

82 Mr.   Missionary at *Oxford,* — 50

83 Mr. *Currie,* Missionary at *Radnor;* 60

84 Mr. *Magaw,* Missionary at *Dover* and *Duck Creek,* — — 40

85 Mr.   Missionary at *Mispillion,* and St. *Paul's* near *Maryland,* — 40

86 Mr. *John Andrews,* Missionary at *Lewes* in *Suffex County,* and at *Cedar Creek,* 40

87 Mr. *Barton,* Itinerant Missionary in *Lancaster,* — — 50

88 Mr.   Itinerant Missionary in the Counties of *York* and *Cumberland,* — — 50

89 Mr. *Murray,* Missionary at *Reading,* 30

North Carolina.

90 Mr. *Earl,* Missionary in *Chowan County,* 50

91 Mr. *Stewart,* Missionary in *Beaufort County,* — — 50

92 Mr.

92 Mr. *Reed*, Miſſionary in *Craven County*,　50
93 Mr. *Thomlinſon*, School-maſter at *Newbern*, 15
94 Mr. *Barnett*, Miſſionary in *Brunſwic County* 50
95 Mr. *Cupples* Miſſionary in ſuch Pariſh as
　the Governors ſhall appoint,　———　} 20
96 Mr. *James Stuart*, Miſſionary where the
　Governor ſhall place him,　———　} 20
97 Mr. *Cramp*, Miſſionary,　———　} 20
98 Mr. *James Macartney*, Miſſionary,　} 20
99 Mr. *John Wills*, Miſſionary,　———　} 20
　where His Excellency Governor *Tryon*
　ſhall be pleaſed to place them.

Georgia.

100 Mr. *Frink*, Miſſionary at *Savannah*,　50
101 Mr. *Ellington*, Miſſionary at *Auguſta*,　40

Florida.

102 Mr. *Thomas Warren*, Miſſionary on the
　Muſquito Shore,　———　———　} 70
103 Mr. *Poſt*, Catechiſt to the *Indians* on the
　Muſquito Shore,　———　———　} 40

Bahama Iſlands.

104 Mr. *Tizard*, Miſſionary at *New Provi-*
　dence,　———　———　} 60
105 Mr. *Baſcome*, School-maſter at *New*
　Providence,　———　———　} 10
106 Mr. *Moſs*, Miſſionary at *Harbour Iſland*
　and *Eleuthera*,　———　———　} 60
107 Mr.　School-maſter at *Harbour Iſland*, 10

Africa.

Africa.

108 Mr. *Philip Quaque*, Miſſionary, Catechiſt and School-maſter to the } 50
Negroes on the Gold Coaſt, —

Total — £4247 10 0

Barbadoes.

109 Mr. *Butcher*, School-maſter at *Co-*
drington College, ——— } 100

110 Mr. *Maſhart*, Uſher in the ſchool,
and Catechiſt to the *Negroes*, } 70

111 Mr. *Denny*, for teaching writing
and arithmetic, ——— } 40

    N. B. Theſe ſalaries are paid out of the
    produce of the plantation.

The Society allow ten pounds worth of
books to each miſſion for a library, and five
pounds worth of pious ſmall tracts to every
new miſſionary, to be diſtributed among his
pariſhioners, and other parcels of books, as occaſion requires. And as the Society generally receive from their miſſionaries regular accounts of
their labours, and of the ſtate of their ſeveral
miſſions, it is thought proper to publiſh the
following abſtract of ſuch informations as were
received from the miſſionaries and others in the
year 1768.

Newfoundland.

Newfoundland.

By a letter from the Rev. Mr. Langman, the Society's Miffionary at St. John's, dated Nov. 3. 1768, it appears, that in the courfe of the year he has baptifed 38 infants, buried 23 corpfes, and married 7 couple. He complains of a great lofs he has fuffered by a fire, which confumed his houfe and all things in it, and the church communion plate, which was kept in his houfe, to the amount of fome hundred pounds. In relief of which the Society have ordered him a gratuity of 50 l.

The Rev. Mr. Coughlan, Miffionary at Harbour Grace and Carboneer, in a letter dated October 15, 1768, fends a furvey of the bay, in which there is no alteration from what he found the preceding year with regard to the number of the inhabitants. In the courfe of the year he has baptifed 46 infants, and 30 adults; has married 5 couple, and buried 16 corpfes. He adminifters the facrament once a month, and has 80 conftant communicants, and on every other Sunday he attends at a chapel which the people have built about five miles from the church. Mr. Jenner has declined the care of the fchool, and Mr. Thurney is placed in his room, and gives general fatiffaction. There are about 30 boys and 12 girls who attend the fchool. The inhabitants have built a very commodious fchool-houfe.

Nova

Nova Scotia.

The Rev. Mr. Wood, Missionary at Annapolis Royal, and Granville, in his letter dated July 9, 1768, acquaints the Society that he was just returned from Halifax, where he had prayed with the Indians at Colonel Goreham's, and performed divine service in Mickmack, and that they understood him perfectly well. That he is making a translation, as fast as he can, of the morning and evening service into Mickmack, and makes no doubt but when he shall have accomplished it, he could instruct any person the Society might appoint to read it distinctly, and with the tone and emphasis peculiar to the language; which he has nearly acquired in less than three months daily application. The Indians behave devoutly during the time of prayer, and after the prayer for the King and Royal Family they bow their heads, and answer, Amen, in their own language.

A letter from Mr. Neuman, School-master at Lunenburgh, dated July 1, 1768, informs the Society that he gives daily attendance to his school, from 8 to 12 in the forenoon, and from 1 to 4 in the afternoon; that the number of his scholars is between 30 and 40; that there are no Indian or negro children in the place, and all the settlers are of the profession of the church of England.

The

The Society are acquainted, by a letter from the Rev. Mr. Eagleſon, Miſſionary to the county of Cumberland in Nova Scotia, dated July 4, 1768, that he arrived on the 27th of June at Halifax, from whence he purpoſed ſetting out immediately for his miſſion, but had expreſs order from the Lieutenant-Governor to repair during pleaſure, to the iſland of St. John, for which place he was to ſail the day following the date of his letter.

Canada.

A letter from the Rev. Mr. Chabrand Deliſle, chaplain to the garriſon at Montreal, dated September 30, 1767, brings the diſagreeable account that the Romiſh prieſts avail themſelves greatly of the neglected ſtate of the church of England in thoſe parts, perſuading the Canadians (who are moſt eaſily to be perſuaded, being a moſt ignorant, bigotted people, and entirely devoted to the prieſts, eſpecially the Jeſuits) that we have not religion ſo much at heart as they. Being deſtitute of a decent place for public worſhip, he is forced to perform it in the Hoſpital chapel. Two Canadians, and one German, have made their recantations. He has baptized within the year 58 children, an adult negro, and an Indian of 7 years of age, and married 22 couple.

G   New

New England.

The Rev. Mr. Arthur Browne, Missionary at Portsmouth in New Hampshire, by a letter of the 6th of November, 1767, informs the Society of the arrival of Mr. Badger, whom he describes to be well calculated for the office of an *Itinerant*, being hardy, strong, resolute, active and diligent, and that he gives universal satisfaction wherever he goes. Mr. Browne's parishioners live in harmony and peace, and increase in number; but the communicants are comparatively few.

There are two letters from this Mr. Badger, the *Itinerant* Missionary in New Hampshire, both dated from Portsmouth; the one of December 17, 1767, the other of August 5, 1768. In the former he writes, that since his arrival in the end of September he had visited every town in the province, where there are any number who belong to the church of England: that they appear well pleased with his administrations, and promise to do all in their power to render his life agreeable, and that the Governor and Mr. Browne give him all the assistance they can. In the second, he mentions a variety of places where he has preached, both on Sundays and week-days: that the distance of the towns is so great, that scarcely any two can attend the
                                                public

public worſhip together, which increaſes the labor of his miſſion, and, as he expreſſes it, keeps him continually on horſeback. The number of ſouls under his care amount to 1132 at preſent, which at his firſt coming did not exceed 740. In leſs than 11 months he has baptiſed 107 children, 1 female adult, and 1 negro. Hitherto he has been obliged to perform divine ſervice, and to adminiſter the ſacrament in private houſes for want of more convenient places.

The Rev. Mr. Bailey, Itinerant Miſſionary on the frontiers of Maſſachuſet's bay, in a letter from Boſton, dated June 27, 1768, takes a modeſt notice of many hardſhips he has undergone in the courſe of his miniſtry, and of the obſtructions to the building a church, which is at length in a way of being accompliſhed, as ſubſcriptions for that purpoſe have been made to the amount of 120l. ſterling.

The Rev. Mr. Wheeler, Miſſionary at George Town and places adjacent, writes, on the 13th of September, 1768, that after a tedious paſſage of ten weeks, he got to Boſton, and, as ſoon as he conveniently could, repaired to George Town, and found the people well diſpoſed to receive him. He has continued to preach among them twice every Sunday to a decent congregation. They have not yet erected a place of worſhip, but ſay they intend it next autumn.

By

By a letter from the Rev. Mr. Weekes, Miffionary at Marblehead, dated June 21, 1768, the Society is informed, that in the courfe of the year he has baptized 49 infants and 1 adult, married 21 couple, and feveral new communicants were added. The number of inhabitants at Marblehead is computed to be 6500, of which one fifth at leaft he believes to belong to the church: the reft are Independents or Congregationalifts; but great harmony fubfifts between him and the Diffenting Minifters.

There are two letters from the Rev. Dr. Johnfon, Miffionary at Stratford and Milford in Connecticut, dated May 9 and November 7, 1768; in the former of which he recommends Mr. John Tyler as a perfon worthy of Holy Orders, of exemplary character, and fufficient learning; having ftudied under Dr. Johnfon, and being a graduate both of the college of New Haven and New York, and fit for the vacant miffion at Norwich. In the latter he recommends Mr. Jofhua Bloomer to the regard of the Society, as worthy to be appointed their miffionary, when he fhall have obtained Holy Orders. He mentions his ill health, and has chofen Mr. Kneeland his affiftant, in order to fucceed him. Since laft Chriftmas he has baptized 18, of which two are adult negroes, and admitted 5 to the communion, of which 2 are alfo negroes; and 2 good families have been added to the church.

The

The Rev. Mr. John Beach, Miffionary at Newtown and Reading, in a letter dated April 4, 1768, writes, that the number of inhabitants exceeds 2000, the greater part of which belong to the church of England. That he has 310 communicants, 15 of which were added to the laft communion : that the church people increafing in thefe parts makes the duty heavy on a fingle clergyman; and the clergy are not likely to increafe till they are bleffed with a refident Bifhop.

By a letter from the Rev. Mr. Clarke, Miffionary at New Milford, Woodbury, Kent, New Fairfield and Sharon of June29, 1768, information is received, that in New Milford there are 92 families of the church, and about 50 communicants : in Woodbury 50 families and 35 communicants : in Kent 65 families and 40 communicants. That fince the 9th of October he had baptifed 60 infants, and 8 adults, one of which was a black. The church in thofe parts is in a very florifhing condition.

New York.

By feveral letters in the courfe of the year from the Rev. Dr. Auchmuty, Rector of Trinity church, and in one from Mr. Livingfton (dated December 20, 1768,) executor of the late Mr. St. George Talbot, it appears that they have met with great trouble in recovering
.the

the legacy left to the Society, which will probably be much lefs than was at firft apprehended, by reafon of many difficulties raifed by the heirs at law, and the obftructions given to the proving the will by them in feveral law proceedings. That the affair is now in a more fuccefsful way, and they hope foon to give the Society fome more certain and pleafing account of it. And the Society are fo well affured of the great pains thefe Gentlemen have taken in this matter, and of their judgment and difcretion equal to their zeal for their fervice, that they efteem themfelves much indebted to them for it, and do return them their hearty thanks. Dr. Auchmuty has recommended the Reverend Mr. Sayer to the miffion of Newburg, to which the Society have appointed him. He writes, that Sir William Johnfon laments the want of clergymen among the Indians in his neighborhood. He has agreed to purchafe the late Dr. Barclay's houfe and farm in the Mohawks country, and intirely acquiefces in a propofal to allot one corner of the farm for a Schoolmafter to build a fmall tenement on it.

The Rev. Mr. Cutting, Miffionary at Hempftead, in a letter of January 7, 1768, fends the Society the following account of his new miffion. That it is a large one, that he thinks the people of his parifh of Hempftead to be civil, hofpitable, and grateful, and mentions one act of their gratitude in building an houfe

at

at their own expence for the widow of their late worthy Miffionary. That his church is large and in general full: the fpot where Mr. Cutting lives is furrounded with Prefbyterians who are kind and obliging neighbors, fober and pious in their converfation, and averfe to religious animofities. Great numbers remain unbaptifed, owing to the principles of Quakerifm, which prevailed there fo long. To the fouth of Hempftead are many inhabitants who are willing to be inftructed, and among whom he frequently officiates on week days: but being a very indigent people they have not the ability to get their children inftructed, nor indeed the opportunity, there being no School-mafter, which he thinks would be a real bleffing in thofe parts. The Society being of the fame opinion, have defired Mr. Cutting to acquaint them at what place he wifhes a fchool to be fixed, and if he can procure a worthy and fit man, he has their leave to employ him. At Oyfterbay the church (which ftill remains unfinifhed) is in general well filled with conftant, ferious and devout people, but not equal in number to thofe of other denominations. Since April he has baptifed 4 adults, and 27 children, and admitted two new communicants. At Flufhing (a vacant miffion) he baptifed one adult and 5 children, and at Huntingdon 4 children.

The Rev. Mr. Munro, lately appointed Miffionary at Albany, returns the Society thanks
for

for that appointment, in a letter of May 2, 1768. He arrived there juſt before laſt Eaſter, and begs leave to aſſure the Society, that he will do every thing in his power to deſerve the good opinion they have conceived of him. He obſerves that Albany is on the communication from New York to Canada, and the metropolis of a very extenſive and floriſhing country whither ſome hundreds of families annually come to ſettle, which gives him hope of adding many to the church. Upon his arrival at Albany he found the church in a poor condition : a ſcattered congregation, reduced to a ſmall number. He has indevored to bring back the people, and reconcile them to their former perſuaſion, by frequent viſiting, and by friendly converſations : and in this he has labored with ſuccefs. In a ſecond letter of the 12th of July, 1768, he writes of the quiet and eaſy ſtate of his congregation, who attend divine ſervice on Sundays very regularly and decently. His communicants were increaſed to 25 to whom he adminiſtered the ſacrament on Whitſunday. He has buried 2 corpſes, and married one couple, baptiſed 9 white, and 4 black children, and two black adults. His catechumens are 30 white children and 12 black adults. To the former he reads prayers conſtantly on Fridays, and ſpends an hour in inſtructing them : the latter he catechizes after evening prayer on Sundays. He offers it as his opinion, that Albany ought to have a reſident clergyman con
ſtantly

ftantly performing his ministerial office there, and the Society are fo fenfible of the neceffity of it, that they intend to appoint a miffionary for the Mohawk Indians, as foon as a proper perfon can be procured.

Mr. Hildreth, School-mafter at New York, in a letter of the 18th of October, 1768, acquaints the Society of the florifhing ftate of his fchool, which confifts of 75 fcholars. In the courfe of a year 13 boys and 7 girls have been put out to trades, &c. and three difcharged for not giving regular attendance. The children are carefully inftructed in the Catechifm, and they make a good proficiency.

New Jerfey.

The Rev. Mr. Odell, Miffionary at Burlington and Mountholly, in a letter dated July 5, 1768, after acquainting the Society that his own congregation give him all the fatisfaction he could wifh, mentions how requifite a miffion is at Waterford and Glocefter, there being at prefent no minifter of the church of England between Burlington and the fouthweft extremity of New Jerfey. Nor lefs requifite does he think it to appoint a miffionary to Trenton, there being no epifcopal church on the great road between Burlington and Brunfwick, a diftance of more than forty miles. The Society have accorded in this matter, and Mr.

H   Lyon,

Lyon, of Taunton has the offer of the mission of Waterford and Glocefter; and as the New Jerfey clergy have recommended Mr. Thomfon, miffionary in Cumberland, to the miffion of Trenton, he has had the Society's leave to remove thither.

The Society have received advice from the Rev. Mr. Abraham Beach, that he arrived fafe at his miffion in the end of September, 1767, where he was kindly received, and found an agreement among all denominations; likewife, that Mr. Ayres arrived fafe at his miffion in April, 1768, and before Michaelmas following had baptized 22 children and 4 adults.

Pennfylvania.

The Rev. Dr. Smith, Provoft of the College of Philadelphia, affures the Society, in a letter of the 22d of October, 1768, that due care is taken of the miffion of Oxford, who have two fermons in three weeks for ten months in the year, and when the Doctor is prevented, Mr. Montgomery fupplies his place, who was regularly educated in the college at Philadelphia, and is reprefented to be an ingenious, ferious, and worthy young man, of 22 years of age. The people wifh him to be their miffionary, and are content to wait for him till he fhall be of proper age for holy orders.

He

He inclofes letters from the miffion of Trenton, backed by recommendation of the New Jerfey clergy, in favor of Mr. Thomfon, who follicits to be removed thither, as does Mr. Andrews of Lewes, from Suffex on Delawar, on account of the unhealthfulnefs of the place, and would gladly accept of York county, and take care of Cumberland too till another miffionery can be got. In this the Society have fo far concurred, that they have given Mr. Andrews leave to remove to the miffion of York and Cumberland, provided he will take the whole duty upon him, as Mr. Thomfon did before, and promife to continue in it without a profpect of having the miffion divided.

A letter from the Rev. Mr. Barton, Itinerant Miffionary in Lancafter, dated Philadelphia, October 18, 1768, brought by Mr. Coombe (whom he recommends to the Society) informs them, that he continues to correfpond with Sir William Johnfon, on the fubject of Indian fchools, a fubject which he hopes the Society will never lofe fight of. There are ftill vacant miffions and difperfed congregations in Pennfylvania, among whom an itinerant miffionary might do infinite good. The people of North Carolina continue to complain of the want of miffionaries. He has lately received a lift of the church people in Rowan county, which amounts to 1500. He returns the Society thanks for the addition

of

of 10 l. to his salary, which, together with the use of a plantation which Governor Penn has been pleased to allow him, will inable him to continue in the service of the Society.

North Carolina.

His Excellency William Tryon, Esq; Governor, in a letter from Brunswick, June 10, 1768, recommends the Rev. Mr. Wills to the Society's regard, and to be incoraged by them to return back again to North Carolina. The Society have accordingly complied with the Governor's desire.

The Rev. Mr. Earl, Missionary in Chowan county, in a letter from Edenton, dated March 26, 1768, acquaints the Society, that since October 1767, he had baptised in his own parish 30 infants, and he has 27 communicants. He has preached to 2 congregations in Berkley parish, and baptized 18 infants; and to 8 congregations in St. Andrew's parish, and baptized there 95 infants, and administered the sacrament to 46 communicants.

The Rev. Mr. Cupples, Missionary in North Carolina, in a letter from St. John's parish, Bute county, April 9, 1768, informs the Society, that he has been inducted, by a commission from his Excellency, into St. John's parish. Since January 1, 1767, he had baptized 382 children, 51 of which were blacks.
He

He has five places to officiate in, at three of which he has adminiftered the facrament four times, to about 60 communicants at each place. There are a few Anabaptifts in his parifh, but the number is decreafing.

Georgia.

The Rev. Mr. Frink, Miffionary at Savannah, writes on Jan. 7, 1768, that he enjoys better health than he did at Augufta, and returns the Society his thanks for the change. In one year he has baptifed 80, buried 120, preached twice every Sunday, and upon the principal holydays always once, befides affording all the affiftance he could to this, and the neighboring province of South Carolina.

The Rev. Mr. Ellington writes, that he got fafe to his miffion at Augufta, on the 12th of November 1767, and was well received. He fays, that there is not one place of worfhip of any denomination within an hundred miles of Augufta either way. He remedies this as far as he can, having been thrice at St. George's parifh ; generally fetting out on a Monday and travelling on that day thirty or forty miles. On the three following days he has performed divine fervice in three different places of the parifh, ten miles wide of each other, and returned home on the Friday. There are two other fettlements over the river Savannah in Carolina,

Carolina, the one about 7 miles diſtant; (where he goes once a fortnight) the other, about 10, (where he goes once a month in the week days) at which places numbers do attend. Since he has been in America he has baptiſed 178 children, and 2 adults, married 15 couple, and buried 12 corpſes. The people are very illiterate, and know little more of chriſtianity than the Indians.

Florida.

Mr. Poſt is arrived on the Muſquito ſhore, but no account yet of his undertaking.

Bahama Iſlands.

The Rev. Mr. Tizard, Miſſionary at New-Providence complains in his letter of June 1, 1768, that the climate ſeems to diſagree with him, and he is apprehenſive that his want of health will hinder his continuing there. Since his arrival he has married 14 couple, buried 19 corpſes, and baptized 73 whites, 9 adult negroes and 5 children. He has 12 communicants. There are on the iſland 253 white men, 264 women, 253 boys, 214 girls, 480 negro men, 358 women, 286 boys, 138 girls.

By a letter of the 27th of February, 1768, the Rev. Mr. Moſs, Miſſionary at Harbour Iſland, and Eleuthera, acquaints the Society, that he arrived at New Providence on the 8th

of

of May, 1767. When he came to Harbour
Ifland, he had at firft a cold reception, from
the people's apprehending that they were to
contribute to his fupport; when they found
that not to be the cafe, they became fond of
him. He performs divine fervice under the
branches of Tamarind trees. The feffions of
Council and Affembly at New Providence,
have enacted a law, which divides Harbour
Ifland and Eleuthera into a diftinct parifh
named St. John's; allows 150 l. current money
out of the Harbour Ifland taxes towards building a church in that ifland, and fettles 50 l.
per annum, Englifh, for falary and houfe rent
for the minifter. From the 8th of May to the
end of the year 1767, he baptifed 71 white,
and 6 black children, 2 black adults, and 1
mulatto child, married 10 couple, and buried
2 corpfes. Communicants are 27, all ferious
good livers.

Africa.

There are two letters from the Rev. Mr.
Philip Quaque, Miffionary, Catechift, and
School-mafter to the Negroes on the Gold
Coaft; the one bearing date October 20, 1767,
the other without any date at all; by which
the Society are informed, that the number of
his fcholars continues the fame. Three of them
read their primmers very well, and moft of
them

them say the catechism as far as the first commandment. But he complains of discoragements which he meets with from the inattention of the garrison to public service on Sundays, and from the Governor himself, who is backward in this particular. On the 2d of August he performed divine service, for the first time, before Cabosheer Cudjo, and many of the Cape Coast people, seemingly to their satisfaction; at which time he expressed again his desire of having an house built containing two long rooms, the one for the service of God, the other for a school. He has since officiated on Sundays, but finds it very difficult to collect them together, as they are ingaged in their idolatrous ceremonies, and addicted to drinking spirituous liquors to excess. The Governor had promised to have his four children baptised, but Mr Quaque has not yet been able to induce him to do so.

Barbadoes.

From several letters from the Society's Officers and Attorneys, at Codrington-College, in the course of the year, the Society is inabled to give the public these informations. That Mr. Mashart, a Gentleman unexceptionable in all respects, is appointed Usher in the college, in the room of Mr. Wharton. That the Attornies in the management of the Society's affairs have

have difcharged their part with the exacteft fidelity, difcretion, labor and zeal; and are moft juftly intitled to the thanks of the Society. Efpecially for their attention and care of the poor Negroes, who have been moft humanely treated. And the Society have given the moft pofitive directions, that befides the greateft tendernefs and care beftowed upon them, no method may be left untried to give them a right fenfe of religion; and that the mafters in particular muft do their utmoft to eftablifh them in all neceffary inftruction.

I

The

☞ The Society, from their first institution, taking into their serious consideration the absolute necessity there is, that those Clergymen, who shall be sent abroad, should be duly qualified for the work, to which they are appointed, desire every one, who recommends any person to them for that purpose, to testify their knowledge, as to the following particulars :

1. The age of the person.
2. His condition of life, whether single or married.
3. His temper.
4. His prudence.
5. His learning.
6. His sober and pious conversation.
7. His zeal for the christian religion, and diligence in his holy calling.
8. His affection to the present Government.
9. His conformity to the doctrine and discipline of the church of *England*.

And the Society do now request, and earnestly beseech all persons concerned, that they recommend no man out of favour or affection, or any other worldly consideration, but with a sincere regard to the honour of almighty GOD, and our blessed SAVIOR; as they tender the interest of the christian religion, and the good of men's souls.

And

And the Society particularly defire their friends in *America* to be fo juft to them, when any perfon appears there in the character of a Clergyman of the church of *England*, but by his behaviour difgraces that character, to examine as far as may be into his *Letters of Orders*, his name and circumftances, and to infpect the public lift of the names of the miffionaries of this Society, publifhed annually with the abftract of their proceedings; and the Society are fully perfuaded it will appear, that fuch unworthy perfon came thither without their knowledge; but if it fhould happen that any fuch fhould come thither from them, they intreat their friends in *America*, in the facred name of Chrift, to inform them, and they will *put away from them that wicked perfon.*

c

I 2   The

The Receipts and Payments on the General Account of the Society for the Year paſt, ſtood
thus at the Audit of the Society on the 26th
Day of *January* 1769.

RECEIPTS.

	l.	*s.*	*d.*
By Ballance of Account in the Hands of the Treaſurer, *Jan.* 27, 1768,	928	3	2
By Benefactions and Legacies and Entrance of Members in the Year 1768, — —	2524	16	11
By Subſcriptions of Members of the Society, — —	578	2	0
By Rent from Tenants, and by Dividends in the public Funds,	1125	15	8

Total 5156 17 9

PAY-

PAYMENTS.

	l.	*s.*	*d.*
For Salaries to Miffionaries, Catechifts, Schoolmafters, and the Officers of the Society,	3824	16	0
For Books, Gratuities to Miffionaries, and other incidental Charges, — —	447	6	8¼
To the Purchafe of 500*l.* Old South Sea Annuities, and Brokerage — —	448	2	6
To Balance due to the Society *Jan.* 26, 1769, —	436	12	6¼
Total	5156	17	9

Abstract of the Society's *London* Account re-
lating to *Codrington* College and their Plantations in *Barbadoes*, as ballanced by the Audi-
tors of the Society, on the 26th Day of
January 1769.

The Society to the Trust Dr.

	l.	*s.*	*d.*
Ballance of Accounts in *January* 1768,	186	15	11½
Nett Produce of 112 Casks of Sugar sold at *London*,	2293	0	0
Dividends on 4000 *l.* Three *per Cent.* Consol. Bank Annuities, due *July* 5, 1768,	120	0	0
Dividends on 3000 *l.* Old South Sea Annuities to the 10th of *October*, 1768,	90	0	0
£	2689	15	11½

The

The Society to the Truft Cr.

	l.	*s.*	*d.*
By Bills drawn by the Society's Attornies, and others, at *Barbadoes*, and paid at *London*,	841	19	5
Salaries to Officers in *London*,	105	0	0
Expence relative to the new purchafed Eftate in *Barbadoes*,	81	9	9
Petty Difburfements —	11	19	9
	1040	8	11
Balance due to the Society on *January* 26, 1769.	1649	7	0½
£	2689	15	11½

A LIST of the

MEMBERS

O F

The SOCIETY *for the Propagation of the Gospel in Foreign Parts.*

Thofe marked thus * were chofen Members in the Year 1768.

A.

THE Right Reverend *Richard* Lord Bifhop of St. *Afaph.*
Charles Ward Apthorp, of *New York*, Efq;
John Apthorp, of *London*, Efq;
James Apthorp, of *Bofton*, Efq;
Eaft Apthorp, M. A.
Mr. *Enos Alling*, of *New Haven, Connecticut.*
Samuel Auchmuty, D. D. Rector of *Trinity Church* in the City of *New York.*
The Rev. Sir *Afhurft Allin*, Bart.
Thomas Afhton, D. D. Fellow of *Eton* College.

K   THE

B.

THE Right Reverend *Edward* Lord Bishop of *Bath* and *Wells*.

The Right Reverend *John* Lord Bishop of *Bangor*.

The Right Reverend *Thomas* Lord Bishop of *Briftol*.

The Honourable *Francis Barnard*, Efq; Governor of the Province of *Maffachufet's Bay* in *New England*.

The Honourable and Reverend *Shute Barrington*, LL. D. Canon Refidentiary of St. *Paul's*.

Richard Barford, D. D.

Edward Ballard, D. D.

Thomas Barnard, M. A. Rector of *Maple Durham, Oxfordfhire*.

The Rev. Mr. *James Barclay*.

Cutts Barton, D. D. Dean of *Briftol*.

John Bradftreet, Efq; Colonel.

Edward Bearcroft, Efq;

George Berkeley, L. L. D. Chancellor of *Chrift's* College, *Brecknock*.

Edward Bernard, D. D. Provoft of *Eton* College.

Jonathan Belcher, Efq; Chief Juftice of *Nova Scotia*.

John Berney, D. D. Archdeacon of *Norwich*.

Calverley Bewicke, Efq;

Thomas Blackwell, M. A.

Ebenezer Blackwell, Efq;

Jonathan Blenman, Efq; Attorney-General in *Barbadoes*.

William

William Bowles, M. A. Fellow of *Winchester* College.

Robert Breton, M. A. Archdeacon of *Hereford.*

Henry Burrough, M. A. Prebendary of *Peter-borough.*

John Burton, D. D. Fellow of *Eton* College.

Philip Brown, B. D.

The Rev. Mr. *Bourdillon.*

Richard Bulkeley, Esq; Secretary of the Province of *Nova Scotia.*

Joseph Banks, Esq;

John Benson, M. A.

Walter Bagot, M. A.

William Bell, D. D. Prebendary of *Westminster.*

William Buller, M. A. Prebendary of *Winchester.*

* *John Bostock,* D. D. Canon of *Windsor.*

C.

THE most Reverend and Honourable *Frederic* Lord Archbishop of *Canterbury.*

The most Reverend *Michael* Lord Archbishop of *Cashel.*

The Right Reverend *Edmund* Lord Bishop of *Chester,*

The Right Reverend *William* Lord Bishop of *Chichester.*

The Right Honourable Lord *Colrayne.*

The Honourable *George Clinton,* Esq; Admiral.

John

John Chapman, D. D. Archdeacon of *Sudbury*.
Timothy Collins, M. A. Canon Refidentiary of
    Wells.
Mr. *John Cobb*.
Edward Codrington, Efq;
John Cookfey, M. A.
Charles Walter Congreve, M. A. Archdeacon of
    Armagh.
Allen Cowper, M. A.
John Craven, M. A.
Lewis Crufius, D. D. Prebendary of *Worcefter*.
Stephen Comyn, Efq;
William Henry Chauncey, Efq;
Colonel *Mordaunt Cracherode*.
Myles Cooper, D. D. Prefident of *King's College*
    at *New York*.
Richard Cuft, D. D. Canon of *Chrift Church*,
    Oxford.

D.

THE moft Reverend *Charles* Lord Arch-
    bifhop of *Dublin*.
The Right Honourable *William* Earl of *Dart-
    mouth*.
The Right Reverend and Honourable *Richard*,
    Lord Bifhop of *Durham*.
The Right Reverend *Charles* Lord Bifhop of
    St. *David's*
The Honourable *Wriothefley Digby*, Efq; LL. D.
Richard Dalton, Efq;

                                    Chriftopher

Christopher Dawson, Esq;

Peter d'Espaignol, Esq;

Samuel Dickens, D. D. Archdeacon of *Durham.*

George Dixon, D. D. Principal of *Edmund Hall* in *Oxford.*

Thomas D'oyly, LL. D. Archdeacon of *Lewis.*

Thomas Drake, D. D.

Robert Dinwiddie, Esq;

David Durell, D. D. Prebendary of *Canterbury.*

E.

THE Right Reverend *Matthias* Lord Bishop of *Ely.*

The Right Reverend and Honourable *Frederick* Lord Bishop of *Exeter.*

Jucks Egerton, M. A.

Richard Eyre, D. D.

F.

FREDERICK *Frankland,* Esq;

   John Fountayne, D. D. Dean of *York.*

Tobias Frere, Esq;

Thomas Edwards Freeman, Esq;

Michael Francklin, Esq; Lieutenant Governor of *Nova Scotia.*

* *Pulter Forester,* D. D. Chancellor of *Lincoln.*

* *Ralph Freman,* D. D. of *Hertfordshire.*

THE

G.

THE Right Reverend *William* Lord Bishop of *Glocester*.

The Right Hon. the Lord *Grosvenor*.

Henry Galley, D. D. Prebendary of *Glocester*.

Edmund Gibson, M. A. Precentor of St. *Paul's*.

Benjamin Goodison, Esq;

John Gooch, D. D. Prebendary of *Ely*.

Thomas Greene, D. D. Dean of *Salisbury*.

Blinman Gresley, M. A.

His Excellency *James Grant*, Esq; Governor of *East Florida*.

Charles Gray, Esq;

H.

THE Right Honourable *George Montague Dunk*, Earl of *Halifax*.

The Right Honourable and Right Reverend Lord *James* Bishop of *Hereford*.

The Honourable and Reverend *John Harley*, M. A. Archdeacon of *Salop*.

The Honourable *James Hamilton*, Esq; Governor of *Pennsylvania*.

Hugh Hall, of *Boston* in *New England*, Esq;

James Hallifax, D. D.

George Harrison, of the City of *New York*, Esq;

Joseph Harrison, Esq; of *New Haven*, *Connecticut*.

Bartholomew Hammond, Esq;

Benjamin

Benjamin Hayes, Esq;

Mr. *George Hayter.*

The Rev. Sir *John Head,* D. D. Bart. Archdeacon of *Canterbury.*

William Henry, D. D.

William Herring, D. D. Dean of St. *Asaph.*

Thomas Herring, M. A.

Samuel Holcombe, M. A. Prebendary of *Worcester.*

Richard Hotchkis, M. A.

Joseph Hudson, Esq; Major General.

William Hutton, L. L. B.

William Hetherington, M A.

John Hotham, D. D. Archdeacon of *Mid-
dlesex.*

The Honourable *Thomas Harley,* Esq; Alderman
of *London.*

Thomas Hollingbery, D. D.

Richard Hind, D. D.

I.

SIR *Edmund Isham,* Bart.

Sir *Stephen Theodore Janssen,* Bart. Chamberlain of *London.*

Charles Jenner, D. D. Archdeacon of *Huntingdon.*

Laurence Jackson, B. D. Prebendary of *Lincoln.*

Samuel Johnson, D. D.

His Excellency *George Johnson,* Esq; Governor
of *West Florida.*

Sir

Sir *William Johnſon*, Bart. his Majeſty's Superintendant for *Indian* Affairs in *North
America.*

Joſeph Jane, B. D.

The Rev. Mr. *Inglis*, of *New York.*

The Reverend *John Jortin*, D. D. Archdeacon
of *London,*

K.

THE Right Honourable *Thomas* Earl of
Kinnoul.

Anthony Keck, Eſq; Serjeant at Law.

Samuel Knight, M. A.

William Knox, Eſq; Agent for *Eaſt Florida.*

Benjamin Kennicott, D. D.

Joſhua Kyte, D. D.

John Kirkman, Eſq; Alderman of the City of
London.

L.

THE Right Reverend *Richard* Lord Biſhop
of *London.*

The Right Reverend *John* Lord Biſhop of
Litchfield and *Coventry.*

The Right Reverend *Jonathan* Lord Biſhop of
Landaff.

The Right Reverend *John* Lord Biſhop of
Lincoln.

The Right Reverend *William* Lord Biſhop of
Londonderry.

The

The Right Honourable the Earl of *Lincoln.*
John Lawrey, M. A. Prebendary of *Rochester.*
William Lloyd, M. A.
Thomas Lloyd, D. D. Dean of *Bangor.*
John Lynch, D. D.
Edmund Lovell, M. A. Canon of *Wells.*
Thomas Lane, Esq;
The Rev. Mr. *Christopher Lonsdale.*

M.

THE Right Honourable *Charles* Lord Viscount *Maynard.*

Margaret Professor of Divinity, *Oxon, Thomas Randolph,* D. D.

Margaret Professor of Divinity, *Cambridge, Zachary Brooke,* D. D.

Alexander Macaulay, Esq;

William Markham, LL. D. Dean of *Christ Church, Oxford.*

Ossory Medlicot, M. A.

John Frederick Miege, D. D. Protestant Ecclesiastical Counsellor to the Elector *Palatine.*

Jeremiah Milles, D. D. Dean of *Exeter.*

John Meyonnet, D. D.

Gideon Murray, D. D. Prebendary of *Durham.*

Roger Mostyn, M. A.

Thomas Moore, D. D.

Charles Morton, M. D. and F. R. S.

John Morgan, B. D. Chancellor of St. *David's.*

Thomas Morison, M. A.

L   *Charles*

Charles Martyn, M. A. of *South Carolina.*
The Honourable *James Murray*, Esq; Governor of all *Canada.*
* *William Morice*, M. A.

N.

THE Right Reverend *Philip* Lord Bishop of *Norwich.*
Gerard Neden, D. D. Prebendary of *Lincoln.*
John Nicols, D. D. Preacher of the *Charter-House.*
——— *Nash*, M. A.
Sir *Roger Newdigate*, Bart.

O.

THE Right Reverend *Robert* Lord Bishop of *Oxford.*
The Honourable *James Oglethorpe*, Esq; Lieutenant General.
Newton Ogle, D. D.

P.

THE Right Reverend *Robert* Lord Bishop of *Peterborough.*
The Right Honourable Sir *Thomas Parker*, Lord Chief Baron of the *Exchequer.*
Vincent Perronet, M. A.
The Reverend *James Perard*, M. A. Chaplain to the King of *Prussia.*
Charles Plumptre, D. D. Archdeacon of *Ely.*
Edward Poole, M. A. Prebendary of *Brecknock.*

John

John Potter, D. D. Dean of *Canterbury.*

John Pownall, Efq; Secretary to the Lords of Trade and Plantations.

The Hon. *Thomas Pownall,* Efq; Governor of *South Carolina.*

Jof. Parfons, M. A.

Charles Pointz, M. A.

The Reverend Mr. *Richard Peters,* Rector of *Philadelphia.*

Colonel *Frederick Philips,* of *Philipfburg* in the Province of *New York.*

William Parker, D. D.

Edmund Proudfoot, Efq;

Beilby Porteus, D. D. Prebendary of *Peter-borough.*

The Rev. Mr. *Provoft,* of *New York.*

Q.

*N*UTCOMBE *Quicke,* LL. B. Chancellor of the Church of *Exeter.*

R.

*T*HE Right Reverend *Zachary* Lord Bifhop of *Rochefter.*

The Right Honourable the Earl of *Radnor.*

Sir *Thomas Robinfon,* Bart.

Regius Profeffor of Divinity, *Oxford, Edward Bentham,* D. D.

Regius Profeffor of Divinity, *Cambridge, Thomas Rutherforth,* D. D.

John Richards, LL. D.

L 2 *William*

William Richardson, D. D. Master of *Emanuel*
   College, *Cambridge*.
William Robinson, Esq;
Mr. *John Ross* of *Philadelphia*.
John Rutherford, M. A.
John Rotheram, M. A.
William Rivet, Esq;

S.

THE Right Reverend *John* Lord Bishop of
   Salisbury.
The Honourable *William Shirley*, Esq; Governor
   of the *Bahama Islands*.
Samuel Salter, D. D. Master of the *Charter-*
   house.
Erasmus Saunders, D. D. Prebendary of *Rochester*.
William Smith, D. D. Provost of the College of
   Philadelphia.
Adlard Squire Stukeley, Esq;
Joseph Sims, M. A. Prebendary of St. *Paul's*.
John Simpson, M. A.
Alexander Steadman, Esq; Chief Justice of the
   Common Pleas in *Philadelphia*.
Sir *William Stephenson*, Knt. Alderman of *London*.
George Stinton, D. D. Chancellor of the Church
   of *Lincoln*.

S I R

T.

SIR *John Thorold*, Bart.
 Thomas Tanner, D. D. Prebendary of *Canterbury*.
John Tatterfall, M. A.
Edmund Tew, D. D.
James Torkington, M. A.
Hugh Thomas, D. D. Dean of *Ely*.
John Thomas, LL. D. Dean of *Weſtminſter*.
John Thornton, Eſq;
Sir *John Torriano*, Knt.
Chauncey Townſend, Eſq;
Thomas Tounſon, B. D.
Barlow Trecothick, Eſq; Alderman of *London*.
Joſiah Tucker, D. D. Dean of *Gloceſter*.
Charles Tarrant, D. D. Dean of *Peterborough*.
John Temple, Eſq; Surveyor General of the Cuſtoms in the North Diſtrict of *America*.
Samuel Turner, Eſq; Alderman of *London*.
John Townſon, Eſq;
His Excellency *William Tryon*, Eſq; Governor of *North-Carolina*.
Edward Tew, M. A.
The Rev. Mr. *Tavan.*

V.

PHILIP *de Valois*, M. A.
 Henry Vane, D. D. Prebendary of *Durham*.
Abbot Upſker, M. A.

         The

The Rev. Mr. *Vaughan*, Chaplain to the Factory at *Hamburgh*.

John Vining, of *Pennsylvania*, Esq;

W.

THE Right Reverend *John* Lord Bishop of *Winchester*.

The Right Reverend *James* Lord Bishop of *Worcester*.

The Right Reverend *Richard* Lord Bishop of *Waterford*.

The Honourable *Benning Wentworth*, Esq; Governor of *New Hampshire* in *New England*.

Francis Walwyn, D. D. Prebendary of *Canterbury*.

Henry Waterland, LL. D. Prebendary of *Bristol*.

John Wilberfoss, Esq;

Christopher Wilson, D. D. Canon Residentiary of St. *Paul's*.

Thomas Williams, of *Merthyr*, Prebendary of *Brecknock*.

Edward Wilson, M. A.

Thomas Wilson, D. D. Prebendary of *Westminster*.

Granville Wheeler, M. A.

Thomas Croome Wickes, D. D.

John Waring, M. A.

George Woollaston, M. A.

George Walker, Esq; Agent for *Barbadoes*.

William Worthington, D. D. Prebendary of *York*.

THE

Y.

THE moſt Reverend *Robert* Lord Archbiſhop of *York*, Lord Almoner.

Francis Yarborough, D. D. Principal of *Brazen-Noſe* College, *Oxford*.

Edward Yardley, B. D. Archdeacon of *Cardigan*.

LADIES

LADIES Annual Subscribers.

LADY *Curzon.*
The Honourable Mrs. *Shirley.*
Mrs. *Cotton* of *Etwall* in *Derbyshire.*
Miss *Cordelia Bright.*
Mrs. *Gordon.*
Mrs. *Sydenham.*
The Honourable Mrs. *George Talbot.*
Mrs. *Elizabeth Torriano* of *Kensington.*
Mrs. *Margaret Floyer,* of *Dorchester.*
Mrs. *Ann Maynard.*
Mrs. *Vic* of *Clifton.*
Miss *Palmer.*

A LIST

A LIST of the

BISHOPS, DEANS, &c.

Who have PREACHED before

The SOCIETY *for the Propagation of the Gospel in Foreign Parts.*

Anno.

1701 THE Reverend Dr. *Willis,* Dean of *Lincoln.*

1702 The Lord Bishop of *Worcester,* Dr. *Lloyd,* not printed.

1703 The Lord Bishop of *Sarum,* Dr. *Burnet.*

1704 The Lord Bishop of *Lichfield* and *Coventry,* Dr. *Hough.*

1705 The Lord Bishop of *Chichester,* Dr. *Williams.*

1706 The Lord Bishop of St *Asaph,* Dr. *Beveridge.*

1707 The Reverend Dr. *Stanley,* Dean of St. *Asaph.*

1708 The Lord Bishop of *Chester,* Sir *William Dawes.*

1709 The Lord Bishop of *Norwich,* Dr. *Trimnel.*

1710 The Lord Bishop of St. *Asaph,* Dr. *Fleetwood.*

1711 The Reverend Dr. *Kennet*, Dean of *Pe-terborcugh*.

1712 The Lord Bifhop of *Ely*, Dr. *Moore*.

1713 The Reverend Dr. *Stanhope*, Dean of *Canterbury*.

1714 The Lord Bifhop of *Clogher*, Dr. *Afh*.

1715 The Reverend Dr. *Sherlock*, Dean of *Chichefter*.

1716 The Reverend Mr. *Hayley*, Canon Refidentiary of *Chichefter*.

1717 The Lord Bifhop of *Hereford*, Dr. *Biffe*.

1718 The Lord Bifhop of *Lichfield* and *Coventry*, Dr. *Chandler*.

1719 The Lord Bifhop of *Carlifle*, Dr. *Bradford*.

1720 The Reverend Dr. *Waddington*.

1721 The Lord Bifhop of *Briftol*, Dr. *Bolter*.

1722 The Reverend Dr. *Waugh*, Dean of *Glocefter*.

1723 The Lord Bifhop of *Ely*, Dr. *Greene*.

1724 The Lord Bifhop of St. *Afaph*, Dr. *Wynn*.

1725 The Lord Bifhop of *Glocefter*, Dr. *Wilcocks*.

1726 The Lord Bifhop of *Norwich*, Dr. *Leng*.,

1727 The Lord Bifhop of *Lincoln*, Dr. *Reynolds*.

1728 The Lord Bifhop of *Hereford*, Dr. *Egerton*.

1729 The Reverend Dr. *Pearce*.

1730 The Reverend Dr. *Denne*, Archdeacon of *Rochefter*.

1731.

1731 The Reverend Dr. *Berkeley*, Dean of *Londonderry.*

1732 The Lord Bifhop of *Lichfield* and *Coventry*, Dr. *Smallbrooke.*

1733 The Reverend Dr. *Maddox*, Dean of *Wells.*

1734 The Lord Bifhop of *Chichefter*, Dr. *Hare.*

1735 The Reverend Dr. *Lynch*, Dean of *Canterbury.*

1736 The Lord Bifhop of St. *David's*, Dr. *Clagget.*

1737 The Lord Bifhop of *Bangor*, Dr. *Herring.*

1738 The Lord Bifhop of *Briftol*, Dr. *Butler.*

1739 The Lord Bifhop of *Glocefter*, Dr. *Benfon.*

1740 The Lord Bifhop of *Oxford*, Dr. *Secker.*

1741 The Reverend Dr. *Stebbing*, Chancellor of *Sarum.*

1742 The Lord Bifhop of *Chichefter*, Dr. *Mawfon.*

1743 The Lord Bifhop of *Landaff*, Dr. *Gilbert.*

1744 The Reverend Dr. *Bearcroft*, Secretary of the Society.

1745 The Lord Bifhop of *Bangor*, Dr. *Hutton.*

1746 The Lord Bifhop of *Lincoln*, Dr. *Thomas.*

1747 The Lord Bifhop of St. *Afaph*, Dr. *Lifle.*

1748 The Reverend Dr. *George*, Dean of *Lincoln.*

1749 The Lord Bifhop of St *David's*, Dr. *Trevor.*

1750 The Lord Bifhop of *Peterborough*, Dr. *Thomas.*

1752 The Lord Bifhop of *Carlifle*, Dr. *Ofbaldifton.*

M 2   1753

1753 The Lord Bishop of *Landaff*, Dr. *Cresset.*

1754 The Lord Bishop of St. *Asaph*, Dr. *Drummond.*

1755 The Lord Bishop of *Norwich*, Dr. *Hayter.*

1756 The Lord Bishop of *Lichfield* and *Coventry*, Dr. *Cornwallis.*

1757 The Lord Bishop of *Chester*, Dr. *Keene.*

1758 The Lord Bishop of *Glocester*, Dr. *Johnson.*

1759 The Lord Bishop of St. *David's*, Dr. *Ellis.*

1760 The Lord Bishop of *Chichester*, Dr. *Ashburnham.*

1761 The Lord Bishop of *Landaff*, Dr. *Newcome.*

1762 The Lord Bishop of *Oxford*, Dr. *Hume.*

1763 The Lord Bishop of *Bangor*, Dr. *Egerton.*

1764 The Lord Bishop of *Peterborough*, Dr. *Terrick.*

1765 The Lord Bishop of *Norwich*, Dr. *Yonge.*

1766 The Lord Bishop of *Glocester*, Dr. *Warburton.*

1767 The Lord Bishop of *Landaff*, Dr. *Ewer.*

1768 The Lord Bishop of *Lincoln*, Dr. *Green.*

1769 The Lord Bishop of *Bristol*, Dr. *Newton*

The Form of a LEGACY to this SOCIETY.

ITEM, *I give to* the Incorporated SOCIETY, for the Propagation of the Gospel in Foreign Parts, *the sum of* . *to be raised and paid by and out of all my ready money, plate, goods, and · personal effects, which by law I may or can charge with the payment of the same* (and not out of any part of my lands, tenements, or hereditaments) *and to be applied towards carrying on the charitable purposes for which the said Society was incorporated.*

N. B. The variation in this form of a LEGACY, from that formerly printed, is made necessary, on account of some unhappy mistakes in wills, by which several considerable legacies have been lost to the Society, and the good intentions of the testators have been intirely defeated, because the sums bequeathed to the Society have been ordered to be raised, or paid out of lands, or real estates, which is not now permitted by law.

Direct to the Reverend Dr. *Daniel Burton,* in *Abingdon Street, Westminster,* their SECRETARY.

And to Mr. *William Symondson,* at the *First Fruits* Office, in the *Inner Temple,* their TREASURER.

www.ingramcontent.com/pod-product-compliance
Lightning Source LLC
Chambersburg PA
CBHW031104020726
47495CB00007B/2039